Po  of Fatherhood Second Edition

Copyright © 2020 by Sowjourn Publishers

All rights reserved.

No parts of this book may be copied or reproduced in any manner whatsoever without written permission of the publisher, except to the case of brief quotations embodied in critical articles or reviews.

Sowjourn Publishers
5962 Wescott Road
Columbia, SC 29212

978-0-9817494-5-7

10 9 8 7 6 5 4 3 2 1

Editor's Note

Everything that happens has a context. That statement is also true of Black fatherhood. We often label a father as "*good*" or "*bad*" without some understanding of the context. That, not surprisingly, leads to an incomplete picture. What role models shaped the person's expectation of what it means to be a father? What types of positive or negative reinforcements influenced his decisions relative to his interactions with his children? Those are just two of the many possible questions that help to give context to how one truly understands the notion of fatherhood.

As I write this, the news is dominated with coverage of the murder of George Floyd and the aftermath of his death. Depending on one's political and cultural orientation, George Floyd was either a "*good guy*" or "*bad guy*". Far too many people were unwilling to leave their opinions of him at the fact that he was the father of 5 children. Like a pack of wolves invigorated with the thrill of the hunt, they had to add their measly two cents on which designations of "good or bad" they were going slap top of the recognized fact that Mr. Floyd was a father. To fulfill their sometimes morbid curiosity, these unsatisfied moral police asked, "*How many women did Floyd impregnate to end up with five children?*" or "*How involved with his children was Floyd when the children were growing up?*" Unfortunately, that is all the context they need to proclaim their judgement on the validity of George Floyd's fatherhood.

I bring up the case of George Floyd because he suffered what a friend referred to as a "*double murder*". First, he was murdered by a sick policeman who showed no sense of humanity as he held his knee against his neck for a tortuous 8 minutes and 46 seconds. Next, George Floyd was murdered a second time when his reputation was destroyed and his past mistakes were highlighted in a sick attempt to justify his killing. Sadly, this double murder phenomenon often occurs when the topic of Black Fatherhood is discussed.

Bad men make bad fathers. That seems to be the first simple-minded assessment many people make on the state of Black fatherhood. Black men are labeled as angry, reckless, uncaring and threatening. These and other negative descriptions affirm in their intellectually empty minds that Black men are bad and hence, Black men are destined to be bad fathers. That is murder one of the double murder of Black fatherhood.

It's bad enough that too many people perceive that Black men lack the inner qualities necessary to interact with their kids in a healthy and wholesome manner. Add to that the notion that Black fathers are absent from the lives of their children and we arrive at the scene of the second murder of Black fatherhood. Black fathers are condemned as not even having the decency show up in their children's lives. First, it is worth mentioning that a recent PEW Research study concluded that Black men are more engaged in the lives of their children than other male racial subgroups. However, let's set that conclusion aside for the moment.

Is there really an unquestioned connection between absenteeism and bad fathering? Simply put, is it possible that a father can not be there physically in the house with the kids, but still be present in their lives? So, maybe *"being absent"* is not as definitive a sign that a father isn't living up to his role as a good parent as many people assume. Next, we need to consider that being absent can be caused by many factors (context). What's the nature of the relationship with the mother? How many fathers are actually involuntarily physically absent from their children (*death, prison, military obligation, health considerations, or economic hardship*)? The conclusion I hope people will conclude from this discussion is that far too many of us rush to judgement when it comes to the topic of this book. Let's not be participants, either conscious or sub-conscious, in the double murder of of the notion of Black fatherhood.

In this second edition of the **Portraits of Fatherhood**, we have the testimony of close to 30 Black fathers which helps to give context to what it means to be a constructive male parent. First let me tell you what this book is not. **Portraits of Fatherhood** is not an idealized and sanitized portrayal of Black fathers. Some of the contributing fathers to this book project are currently married to the mother of their children and some are not. Some of these men are active in the lives of children with whom they are not the biological fathers and some came late to the party. Some of these men had to figure out how to be a good father to their children while being physically absent. Others have had to stay true to their high expectations of fatherhood while they negotiated a less than amiable relationship with the mother. Most of these writers made mistakes and many took a long time to recognize and fix their missteps. This book is full of examples of ordinary men making ordinary decisions and sometimes making ordinary errors on their respective journeys of fatherhood.

Now on to what this book is. **Portraits of Fatherhood** is a collection of essays that provides sneak peaks into what it takes to be a Black father. The men who wrote the essays included in the second edition speak from their experiences. Some give direct advice on how to have a positive influence in the lives of their children. Others plainly lay out their observations and leave it to the reader to draw their own conclusions. These men are not necessarily experts on fatherhood even though they may be experts in their respective careers. Their mastery of the many facets of being a father is based on the ups and downs of fatherhood and the conclusions they've drawn from these ups and downs.

So, if you are genuinely interested in gaining a more comprehensive understanding of African-American paternity, this book is a good place to either start or continue that process. In their diverse styles, the men who contributed these essays are adding texture to the portrait of Black fatherhood. Their statements, self-confessions, expressions of guilt or hope or pride all help to paint a picture of an often misunderstood topic. These men provide a vigorous defense against the attempted double murder of the viability and relevance of African-American fatherhood. Far too many Black men have been charged with being at best, an inadequate parent and at worse, a bad father. These false complaints are often based on a lack of context. The intellectual laziness of these accusers is on display each time they level their charges. Countering that false and misleading depiction of Black fatherhood, this book presents an alternative version of the reality of being a father of African descent; the good, the bad and the ugly.

Kevin Morgan - Editor

Table of Contents

Essay Title	Author	Page
MAN-UP!	Dr. Timothy Tee Boddie	1
How Do I Portray Fatherhood	Oscar J Walker, III	6
A Father's Legacy	Kevin E. Wimberly	11
Hero Mine (Poem)	Terry E. Carter	15
Fatherhood	Dana O'Banion	21
Being There	Billy Coker	26
Words of Wisdom	Michael R. Twyman, Ph.D.	29
Just As I Am	Dr. Robert Martin	34
Blessed To Be A Blessing	Marty Bulger	39
A Statement on Friendship to Sons	Dathon O'Banion	42
007: A Lesson in Life	Richard T. Benson, Sr.	45
One Hundred Words on Fatherhood	Gregory A. Montgomery II	54
Blessed Fatherhood	Reggie Dokes	56
Fatherhood: A Sacred Responsibility	Rev. Dr. Gary A. Williams	58
Real Fathers	Dr. Omari Daniel	64
The Least….	Kevin Morgan	67
What's The Matter With White People?	Kenneth M Moore	71
Stability	Rev. Levonia Belt	81
Two Homes, One Heart	Carlos Jones	85
A Better Portion	Bruce Strouble	89
Developing The Father In You	Rev. James Gladden	93

Fatherhood	Milton Jones	97
A Father's Test of Faith	Jerome S. Nesbitt	100
The Reluctant Father	Irvin A. Walker	104
Letter To My Son	Rev. Torrey Woods	110
Never Knew My Father	John Sells	111
A Portrait of Fatherhood: Commitment, Engaged, and Loving	Dr. Nikolai Vitti	113

August 2020

Thornhill & Minnie,

Thank you for your example of excellence & dedication to your family & friends. You continue to be an inspiration.

Blessings,
Robert

MAN-UP!
Dr. Timothy Tee Boddie

In the vernacular of the day, the phrase "Man Up" has become popular as a way to encourage men to be masculine and to be manly. It has come to mean different things to different people under different circumstances, but it sends searing shots of testosterone to men who have acted weak, soft, or effeminate. Most men I know, including me, have been raised on this notion that real men don't cry. When we get hurt, we are admonished to "suck it up!" Many of us never learn how to express our feelings verbally.

This can become a problem. The problem with this mixed message is that, to some, it implies that to be a man, one should never present himself with stereotypical feminine characteristics, lest he be written off as a "wuss," a sissy, or a punk--someone who can be used, abused, misused, maligned and/or marginalized. To others, it may send a message that, to be a man, one must be more aggressive or commandeer a situation in which others don't know what to do. To still others, it may inadvertently become an excuse to be completely unemotional, uncommunicative, or worse, to engage in domestic violence.

When I use the term, "man up," it connotes gender-neutrality—one that reflects what I learned from my own father, who was my standard for what it means to be a man. This term "man up" is best reflected in the familiar biblical narrative of Abraham and Isaac. As I look at this text, I see that God has given us a glimpse of what it means to be a good father, but also, what it means to MAN UP!

The first thing this story teaches us is that in order to "man up," a man must first be willing to show up! In the space of only 14 verses, Abraham's name is called three times:

    1) God calls him.

    2) Isaac calls him.

    3) And an angel calls his name.

And each time he is called, Abraham responds, "Here I am." In other words, he showed up!

Someone has said that 75% of success in life is simply showing up! Even though my late father was a busy pastor and was raised "old school," he always found a way to show up for my brother, sister and me, when it counted most. Whether it was for a football game, a dance recital, a concert or whatever, Daddy would be right there whenever he could, and sometimes, he sacrificed time away from his parishioners to be there for us. I am often mystified when men reach for excuses for not being available to their children. When it comes to being a good father, the very least a dad can do is show up! You never know what a powerful and positive impact we make on our children for just being there to support, to encourage, to cheer, and to motivate them to "keep on keeping on!"

In this text, Abraham showed up to God, so he was spiritually available. He also showed up to Isaac, making him emotionally available. And he showed up to the angel of the Lord, so he was theologically available. So, if you really want to man-up, be like Abraham and show up!

Secondly, to "man up" means not only to show up, but also to listen up! This text clearly shows that Abraham not only showed up, but he also listened up to everyone who called on him. He listened when God told him to take his son Isaac up to the mountain and prepare him for a sacrifice. No protest, no resistance, no excuses. Isn't that amazing?! That tells me one thing: to "man up" also means to listen up. But to listen up sometimes means to be obedient!

That may seem counter-intuitive, but theologian and educator, Parker Palmer points out that the word "obey" comes from the Latin root word "audere," the same word from which we get our word for "audio," which means "to hear." So, the original meaning of the word "obey" literally meant "to hear" or "to listen." Sometimes, we men need to learn not only to show up, when & where we are expected, but also to listen up (and be obedient), when and where it's needed! Isaac asked his father,

"…but where is the wood for the burnt offering?" That was a question that demanded a careful and discerning listening ear, in light of the fact the only thing left to sacrifice for a burnt offering was Isaac himself!

I'm reminded of a time a few years ago when I was watching a football game, one of my favorite pastimes. And my wife came into the family room and started talking to me about an important decision she was about to make. Now, this was a Redskins/Dallas rivalry game, so it took me a minute to tune in. After she talked for about a short while, she realized I hadn't even looked her way, so she stopped mid-sentence and said,

"Tee, are you listening to me?"

So, I pretended I had been listening all along and replied, "Yeah baby, I'm listening to you; heard every word you said."

Of course, you know she didn't believe that. Here's the thing though: She didn't want me to solve her problem, resolve her dilemma or fix her issue. My wife just wanted her husband to listen to her. In that moment, she just wanted to be heard!

Finally, this story reveals that we must also learn to Look up! When you're going through some difficulty, if you're looking down, when you're going through, you can only see the valley! But, when you're going through the valley, you can only see the mountains, if you look up!

The text says that when Abe and Isaac came to the place where God had told him to go, he looked up! The key to walking into the place where God has led you is to LOOK UP!

When he looked up, suddenly, an angel of the Lord shouted out from Heaven, Abraham, Abraham!" This time not only did Abraham show up. Not only did he listen up. But, once again, at the sound of his name, Abraham looked up! Essentially, the angel was saying, "Abraham had passed the test! God just wanted to see if Abraham would trust God enough to go all the way!"

To "man up," then, means that in all relationships, REAL men show up, listen up, and look up, and recognize that the only true sacrifice is the sacrifice of self!

How Do I Portray Fatherhood?
Oscar J Walker, III

Our son, Oscar Jermaine Walker was born July 31, 1975. The Lord allowed us, (Sarah Jane Fleming Walker and I) to be guardian over this beautiful baby boy. Of course, prior to our son's birth, we had received advice from both sides of the family and friends on how to bring up a child (girl or boy).

Below is a list of experiences we had in raising Jermaine. From my perspective, it was a team effort. Each one of us playing our role in raising him. Of course, we shared many experiences – below are just a few:

Experience 1

I was raised by my grandfather and grandmother. My grandfather was active in the church. He was a Deacon and Moderator of the local Church Association. I accompanied him when he moderated the Association meetings. When he attended other meetings, he wanted me to go with him. Little did I know, my grandfather (Deacon Eugene L Longshore) was mentoring me. That really stuck with me. I carried that experience over to my son. I remember attending a Brotherhood meeting at my church and my son came along with me. I will never forget – one brother asked me, how did you get your son to come to brotherhood meetings? My response was he did not have a choice.

When Jermaine received his driver's license, I informed him that it would be unacceptable to me if he received one ticket for speeding or a violation. I wanted him to never think this would be okay. If he got a ticket, I would have responded by making him surrender his license to the Division of Motor Vehicles. With achievements, comes responsibilities. I wanted him to learn that lesson early in life. He went through high school and college without a traffic violation. I really should say – no tickets that I know of because it was never reported to the insurance company.

Experience 2

This bundle of love brought us closer to each other. We believe that Jermaine was a blessing and not a burden. My career started in Newberry, SC. Sarah's career was in teaching and she transferred to the Newberry County School System. One of our long-time friends of the family (Mrs. Sally Glacier) wanted to keep Jermaine. The reason I bring this up is because if we were late picking him up after going out, Mrs. Sally would not release Jermaine to us in the winter season because of the weather. That is one of the most memorable times in Jermaine's early years. We were blessed to have her because we were taught how to care for a child.

Experience 3

Sarah and I frequently discussed methods and ways on how to bring Jermaine up. One early rule was exposing Jermaine to what we called simple "house etiquette".

Things placed on the "coffee table" like candy, glass fixtures, cabinet doors, etc., were described to our son as "do not touch" items. We can recall when children were visiting our home, they would wander all over our home touching things. They would say things like, "I want candy" or "I want this", etc. We did not have that problem when we visited friends' home with Jermaine. He was accustomed to things being around that he could not touch. He was trained at an early age to not disturb things just because they attracted his attention.

Experience 4

Since Sarah was teaching in another area, I was responsible for taking Jermaine to school and back. We wanted the school to see me in case there were any concerns on grades, discipline, etc.
I informed him that if any situation came up in school, that I was going to believe the teacher first. Whatever it was, our goal was to support the teacher unless some other obvious situation occurred. Throughout his 12 years in school, we had no challenging situations.

Experience 5

As parents, we had many conversations with God about the raising of Jermaine. Our prayer was for him to know God early in life. If anything happened to us in his early years, he would know that he could go to God for his strength. We wanted him to be well-rounded, knowing how to interact with all youths his age. When he was playing basketball in the neighborhood, I noticed a change in his attitude and personality when he came home. Obviously, this came from the different influences he faced with the neighborhood boys. Knowing that I wanted to play a positive role in this situation, I had a half court concrete pad poured in my backyard for Jermaine and his friends to play basketball. I informed him to tell his friends to come play ball in our backyard. Little did he know that this was part of my plan to meet his friends. I sometimes would fix snacks and drinks for them. This would give me an opportunity to meet "the good, the bad and the ugly". Not only was this rewarding, the kids felt safe playing not worrying about older kids trying to dominate the game. We were also able to carry on different discussions about life, responsibility, individual attitudes, etc.

In Conclusion

Currently, Jermaine lives in Charlotte, NC. He is a graduate of Winthrop University. He purchased his own home two years after finishing college. He worked for 10 years as a head basketball coach. He is now in the classroom as a teacher working on his Master's to become a high school principal.

In my opinion, a male child needs a father, mentor or someone with strong influence to guide him. We love our women; however, a woman does not have that male voice and the command that God has granted men. I truly feel that there is a special assignment for Black males as role models. Society has a strategic plan for Black males and that's incarceration. The only avenue that's on the table is for Black males and mentors to address this issue head-on. We must help our young males by offering workshops, activities and opportunities that place Black males and mentors in the classroom as early as the third grade.

No other group or organization is going to mentor our Black males on the way they should go. It has to come first from the home, community, the church and groups interested in exposing our Black males toward God's Master Plan and that's to serve Him.

A Father's Legacy
Kevin E. Wimberly

Growing up my parents told me it should be my goal to achieve more than what they achieved in their lifetimes. As successful educators, community activists, mentors, missionaries, and exceptional parents, they did not make the bar one that would be easy for me to hurdle. It started with my Dad, E. Kevin Wimberly. Both of my parents were leaders, but my father set the standard. Looking back, that standard was set by his father, Ezekiel Wimberly, and my mother's father, Rev. Jackson Simmons. Given what my mother, Blanche S. Wimberly, saw in her father, she wanted her mate to have the same characteristics and traits. One who was God fearing, God loving, had a strong work ethic, a disciplinarian, a provider, and a protector. Also, a man that was witty, humble, and valued family bonding time.

I did not have to go outside of my home or my family to find positive role models. While some would say I was spoiled to have these influences in my life, I viewed them as a blessing. Don't get me wrong, I had uncles and other male mentors who also were positive role models. But it was this trio, my father and both grandfathers, who I believe made me into the man I have become and want to continue to be. My father and grandfathers made it look easy to accomplish all that they did. Growing-up, I did not realize the life lessons that I was experiencing and would need later in life with my children.

My grandfathers were both farmers in rural Aiken County on the Aiken and Barnwell County line of South Carolina in a community known as White Pond. I recall hearing the stories that have been passed down from generation to generation how White Pond was a tight knit community where everyone looked out for each other. Not only were seeds being planted to produce a harvest for income and nourishment, but also seeds of discipline, a strong work ethic, accountability, and responsibility. The children would see how their parents provided for them. They also had responsibilities on the farm so there would be be food to eat and clothes to wear. They also would learn the importance of sharing with others who didn't have much when the harvest was plentiful. My mother's family was pretty large with18 children, but even then, they always shared.

This rearing and upbringing would manifest itself in my father. He was one who always remembered where he came from. Upon graduating high school, he furthered his education at Livingstone College in Salisbury, NC, and obtained his education degree. He would use this to enter the education field in the middle 1970's. My father became one of the first African-American males to teach kindergarten in the public schools of the Union County School District in North Carolina. Those seeds that had been planted in-him throughout his childhood would blossom and allow him to start planting seeds in-the many children that he would encounter over the next 30 years of his career. Although, I was the only biological child of my parents, they would love, discipline, nurture, and cherish many more children. As those children would grow and mature, they would tell my parents how much they appreciated what they did for them during that time in their life and how they made a difference.

Not only did my dad work as an educator, he worked a few part-time jobs early in his education career. He also earned his Masters in Human Development and Learning (MHDL) from the University of North Carolina, Charlotte as well as his Principal Certification. He wanted the best for our family. After his death, my Aunt Cynthia and I were talking about my dad and she remembered how he worked several jobs. She recalled asking him how many jobs he was going to work and he replied, "However many it takes". That goes back to what was instilled in him as child. He made it look easy during my childhood. He still spent time with me and our family as I don't ever remember him missing a sporting event, school or church program, piano recital, or band performance. In fact, he would drive the activity bus for the band during my high school years. This was in addition to his church and community organizations activities.

Since his passing in June 2016, I have come to appreciate his life more than ever. During his time here on Earth, I appreciated his influences on me then. But as I remember all he has accomplished as a husband, father, grandfather, son, brother, uncle, teacher, and friend, I am even more amazed. My twin daughters, Kyla and Koryn and youngest daughter, Khloe, were a delight to their grandfather, my dad. He really enjoyed spending time with them as much as they enjoyed spending time with him. It was his goal to see them grow-up into amazing adults. Sadly, that will not happen physically on earth, but spiritually, he is looking down on them and smiling. The torch has been passed to me to take on this amazing legacy and it is my goal to pass it on to my children. The race is not easy, but I continue to strive to do my best. I know it was not easy for my grandfathers and father, but those seeds that were planted in them blossomed and the seed that has been planted in me is being blossomed. The life experiences I remember in my childhood, I am trying to instill in my daughters. It is my hope the characteristics and traits my grandfather and father portrayed, I will be able to live up to. I pray they will seek to find a mate later in life that will possess these same characteristics.

Hero Mine
Terry E. Carter

I've always believed in heroes...
Collected comic books by the dozens--
Spidey, Fantastic Four, Thor, and Black Panther.
Watched the Dark Knight,
serialized in sepia tone at the Regent Theatre.
Played Batman's sidekick Robin,
alongside Billy Vargus on the stage
at Hobbs Jr. High...
White tights, died Kelly green
and a brown felt mask.
I strutted and believed
and it got in me.

I watched Joe Friday--
"Just the facts, ma'am..."
and Bruce Lee—
"It's like a finger pointing to the moon.
If you concentrate on the finger,
you'll miss all that heavenly glory!"
and James Tiberius Kirk—
"Scotty, beam me up!"
and Sidney Poitier—
"They call me Mr. Tibbs."
I watched and believed
and it got in me.

I saw JFK, and RFK,
and Malcolm, and Medgar and Martin
live for a principle in danger
and a people in bondage.
They asked not...
They climbed to the mountaintop...
They suffered the slings and arrows...
They studied war, hurt, pain and oppression.
They died, awash in the blood of conviction.
I learned and believed
and it got in me.

I've always believed in heroes…
larger than life cats that
lit up the sports pages—
Satchel Paige and Jackie Robinson,
Jim Brown and Joe Louis,
Gale Sayers and Jesse Owens,
Hammerin' Hank, the "Say Hey Kid" and Sweetness.
the Sugar Rays…
the Michael J's…
the KC Monarchs…
and the Homestead Grays—
I cheered and I believed
and it got in me.

I watched the Louisville Lip

talk that trash one that day,
then jab and hook and smash, for pay
and a heavyweight crown as Cassius Clay—
But titles were lost to a prison stay,
defending his own beliefs.
"Got no quarrel with them Viet Cong..."
So objecting conscientiously,
to the killer his country said he should be,
instead he became
Muhammad Ali.
I marveled and I believed
and it got in me.

I heard musical magicians.
The regal, the elite,
Black and tan fantastic—
the Duke, the Count, King Oliver
Miles, Trane, Bird and Monk,
jazz Giants, lyrical lions...
Heard the Motown Sound,
Memphis Groove and Philly Soul...
Isaac, and Luther, Donny Hathaway
Marvin Gaye, Billy Paul, Grover
and the Godfather.
I listened and believed
and it got in me.

I always believed in heroes.

I really never had to look very far
to find one.
Never had to leave
my house and my street
and my own backyard.
Watched a good man
love his wife and children,
tend his garden,
sow a seed and reap a harvest.
I've grown and believed
'cause it's in me.

I watched my daddy.
People up here in the North
seldom pronounced his name right.
It's Varnie, not Vinnie, or Barney.
Pronounced his name wrong sometimes,
but never in nastiness or disrespect.
It's just that he was so much a
Southern gentleman
in such a decidedly northern space.
Such a Southern gentleman…
I watched and believed
and it got in me.

I watched him plaster a thousand ceilings.
He did things the old-fashioned way—
built his own staging with wooden crates

and heavy planks.
Gypsum lath and slacked lime and
silica sand…
expertly applied to pine strapping
over bone straight studs, 16" on center.
The hammer and the nail
the mason's hawk and trowel,
I lugged and believed
and it got in me.

I always believed in heroes.
Never had to look very far
to find one.
Never had to leave
my house and my street
and my own backyard…
Watched a good man
love his wife and children,
tend his garden,
sow a seed and reap a harvest.
I've grown and believed
'cause it's in me.

And I smile now…
on this day when my first hero
is going home to be with God the Father.
Because I know that
the first hero I ever believed in,

is the first hero
that ever believed in me.

Dedicated to my Dad, Varnie Carter, RIP, December 16, 2014

©2014, Terry E. Carter, from the 2016 Xulon Press book, "Brown Skin and the Brand New Day, A Poet's Renaissance", reprinted with express permission from the author.

Fatherhood
Dana O'Banion

Difficult and yet so rewarding. There's no manual for this thing called fatherhood. Even if there was, I'm pretty certain that it wouldn't be applicable to all children. What might work for one child is not guaranteed to work for another not even in the same household. My two sons are very different and I understood this early on. My oldest son has been a prolific reader since about age three and my youngest took to math without even really ever acknowledging he was into math.

That said, those were the good old days that seem a distant memory. Long gone are the days when you would take your little leaguers to practice in the park and afterwards they would say "*daddy why don't you play pro baseball?*" They believed the fly balls you hit to them travelled home run distance and you were worthy of the pros.

In their eyes, you were the closest thing to being a super hero. When you arrived home from a day's work, your little ones would enthusiastically greet you as you crossed the threshold.

Fast forward to their teen aged years and the adoration you felt seems fleeting. They continue to develop into little individuals and their personalities and independence blossom. Their "*friends*" seem to take over.

The four years of high school goes like that! You continue to attempt to instill values, morals and lessons that you believe in and that will assist them in their maturation. Then bam, you are preparing to send them off to college.

When I dropped my eldest son off at his Ivy league institution, I felt as if I failed to impart lessons over the high school years. Not that I hadn't shared any but the conversations I played out in my mind never occurred. So, when I sat with him moments before I was to leave him in the shadows of ivy, I boo hoo'd like a baby (worse than the time I dropped him off for nursery school, go figure). I was overwhelmed by dropping him off miles away from home and feeling I failed to prepare him. Ultimately, I had to trust that I provided him a strong foundation. By all accounts, he is doing well so I guess my worry was unfounded.

Well, my youngest son wasn't so fortunate. Since his brother left for college, I took every opportunity I've had over the past two years to instill a lesson. For me, part of parenting is being relentless and repetitive in the things I value. I value education, so my sons have been deluged daily with my thoughts on learning since kindergarten.

One of the most difficult experiences that I had as a father was sharing bad news with my youngest son. He was midway through his junior year when I received a text indicating that he would have to see a doctor after school as he believed he had dislocated his knee. He injured his knee while practicing his favorite sport, baseball. An emergency room and doctor visits led to crutches and an MRI. We'd like to protect our family from harm but it ain't always possible.

My wife called me at work with the results of my son's MRI - torn meniscus (a bucket handle tear, no doubt). My wife and I decided to share the results with him later that night at dinner. We informed him that the results were in and his knee would require surgery as soon as possible. My son asked about his baseball season and I informed him, based on everything I read, his recovery would be about three months. That conversation was difficult for me as I watched how my response to his question dampened his spirits. I tried to cheer him by suggesting that we wait to see what the doctor had to say the next day about his recovery.

The next day we met with his surgeon. It was confirmed that the baseball season was over. His doctor was very upbeat about the recovery and said he would definitely play soccer and his favorite sport baseball again.

The surgery went well (in the words of his surgeon, "perfect"). My son followed the doctor's orders and began an ice and motion regimen that he had to complete every day, three times a day. Each day I felt like I was in therapy too as I had to set up his continuous motion and ice machine before school, after-school and late night right before bed. I learned a lot about my son during his recovery. He was upbeat and took to the challenge of recovery with vigor. I learned about his perseverance, a trait that I've always attempted to instill in him. I observed him through the pain, the physical therapy and the late nights and early mornings complete homework and continue to excel in school. Observing the lessons that I instilled in him manifest during this trying time was quite rewarding.

Ultimately, my son's recovery was complete and he was given the green light by his doctor to play on the last game of the season. Although he didn't play in that game, his recovery and return to baseball was complete. Although I still worried about the possibility of re-injury, I was ecstatic for my son's recovery.

Finally, recall I mentioned teen aged years and the fleeting adoration one feels. Well, it's funny because you sometimes just don't realize the impact you've had or are having. My youngest son certainly doesn't let on.

Recently my wife and I attended a scholarship awards banquet for my youngest son. He couldn't attend because he had a baseball game. When we arrived at the banquet, we were greeted by a woman who interviewed my son for the scholarship. She spoke highly of him and shared with us that when she interviewed him, she asked him "who was his role model?" He answered, "my dad". Jackpot! As I said earlier, fatherhood is so rewarding.

Although filled with ups and downs, this little revelation is what makes fatherhood so rewarding and worth every minute.

Being There
Billy Coker

Webster definition of fatherhood says, *"the state of being a father"*. I am blessed to be the father of two beautiful and intelligent daughters. When our first daughter was conceived, our doctor said we should not only pray for a healthy child but also an intelligent child. That really resonated with me because God blessed us to have children and I began to feel the pressure of being a father. I've never done this before, there are no rule books on being a father. So, I did what came naturally. I prayed to my Heavenly Father. I then began to reflect on my upbringing and on the impact of the men that were in my life; my father, my friends' fathers, my teachers, coaches and mentors. But it wasn't until I prayed to God that I received the answer to my questions that I posed to Him; *"Be there"*.

In today's society of absentee fathers, especially in the African-American home, being there was most important. So being obedient, I strongly focused on being there for my children. As a former athlete, I had to get in the game to play the game. Fatherhood is not a spectator sport. By being there, I have witnessed some wonderful, not so wonderful, the good, the bad and the ugly events of life. My presence was most important for the growth of my children and for their mother. Being there forced me to do something. Be it right or wrong, I realized as their father that it was my responsibility to nurture, provide and protect my girls. Those responsibilities extended to their mother!! They needed to know ~~that~~ their daddy would be there for them. You see, being there for the birth of my children was so awesome. I was overwhelmed to see God's miracle unfold! I promised to be there when their mother was just too tired. I was determined to be ~~Being~~ there when they needed to be rocked to sleep (*rock rock was a special time in our house*). I would stop everything to rock my girls to sleep. Say "*rock rock*" to my girls even now and they will simply smile. I will always treasure being there for that first step and that first swimming lesson as an aqua tot. Say "*motorboat*" and they will smile again. Being there for that first day of school and taking photos of them on that special day was awesome. It was a family tradition for years. Being there at the first dance recital, heel and toe was our cry. Being there as they performed on stage from pre-school to college was very special. Being there at school for them was very important.

Unfortunately, in most homes today, it's the mother who handles school problems or concerns. They usually are the ones who are present on field trips, sporting events or being their number one cheerleader. Well, in our family, mom really was their number one cheerleader.

As the father of my girls, I enjoyed being there for their spelling bees. Oh my God, I never felt so much pressure. I took my daughters on their first date. It was later revealed that my presence or being there at the school kept them from having dates on a regular basis. See how being there works! I'm proud to say I was there for the ups, the downs, the good, the bad, and the ugly.

The most important compliment I've ever received was from my wife, the mother of our daughters. She told me that I'm a good father. I thank God for revealing and showing me that being there is the key.

Words of Wisdom
Michael R. Twyman, Ph.D.

The words of wisdom I am inspired to impart come in a season of being a father of a 16-year old teenager and a 35-year-old man. I often remind my sons that I maintain a distinct advantage over them. I have the lived experience of once being their ages and possessing a very vivid memory of what my life was like during those stages of my development. And though we agree the world has changed dramatically since I was their ages, the wise King Solomon concluded there is nothing new under the sun. All the challenges, temptations, snares, and pitfalls confronting their paths were in existence during my earlier years and remain present to some degree in my daily walk.

Even still, I have come to know the many freedoms, joy, fulfillment, and dignity that comes with living a life with **purposefulness** and **self-discipline**. I believe mastering these traits can best determine the quality and trajectory of one's life. However, let me be the first to confess that I have yet to perfect leading my life with clarified purpose and unwavering self-discipline. I often fall short and attempt to share with others when I miss the mark, especially with my sons and the young people I mentor. Each day we are given another measure of grace and a new opportunity for us all to be better than we were the day before.

As I mature and grow in my faith journey, I truly believe that men are uniquely positioned to teach and model these attributes to their sons in ways that a mother may not be able to do so. Having lost my mother quite a few years ago, I would also venture to say I did not truly understand and accept what it meant to be a man until I was forced to be emotionally independent and accountable when I could no longer lean on the one person who always had my back. The mother-child bond forms in the womb, and the covering she instinctively gives to her children is not fully appreciated by them until it is taken away.

Oftentimes, fathers must work harder to establish and define their relationships with their children. The father-son relationship probably requires the most work. After all, males may have ego and competition issues with one another which are difficult to admit and rein in, and often stand in the way of showing our authentic selves to each other. Thus, the strong embrace, a kiss on the forehead, or an encouraging word can go a long way in affirming our children's value and help them to make smarter choices.

My eldest son found himself in a situation recently where his lack of foresight and judgment resulted in him losing his job. This job was one where he had distinguished himself as a highly competent and respected team member and an asset to the organization. Unfortunately, he briefly dated an adult student who was also a scholarship beneficiary of his department. However, in his professional capacity, he had no authority or oversight for awarding or administering the scholarship. He failed to consider the implications of such a relationship by just mere perception, but he was smitten by the young lady's interest in him. His decision to date her followed a recent break-up with another woman to whom he was engaged to marry.

In the end, despite no legal or written company policy precluding such a relationship, he was terminated without cause. This outcome was devastating and had him questioning everything about his ability and future career. It is worth noting that the young lady disclosed to his employer she was uncomfortable about her relationship with my son because of his professional position only after they stopped seeing each other.

Soon after this occurrence, my high school sophomore received his first (and hopefully last) out-of-school suspension for inappropriate use of his hands with a female classmate. He maintains that the interactions were consistent with how they have routinely played and kidded with each other in the past. She communicated to her parents and subsequently to the school dean that she felt threatened enough to refrain from coming to school the next day after their exchange. She feared my son would seek some retribution for telling on him. This incident followed an online exchange with him and other boys that involved another girl who felt exploited due to compromising photos of her that my son was privileged to view via Snapchat.

My wife and I are sensitive to all the stereotypes and cultural dynamics of our son being an African American male athlete in a predominately White, private school that may be at work in this case. Furthermore, we are not certain he fully comprehends how he is being played in a game that was never designed for him to win. Without sending a message of victim-hood, we want to instill in him a heightened sense of self-control that will ultimately lead him to have greater liberties.

So, what is the life lesson to be learned from both scenarios? First, the Bible teaches us that everything that is lawful is not expedient or prudent. Second, since Adam and Eve in the Garden of Eden, mankind has been faced with honoring God or himself. We know, trust, and believe that our purpose as Black men is far greater than what the world has to offer us. The more we can pause, think, and contemplate the potential consequences of our choices, the more power and control we will have over our lives and our destinies.

Experience has taught me straying ever so slightly from the Lord's direction and yielding to my own lusts and desires is when Satan has the best chance to undermine what God has called me to do. My prayer for my sons and other young Black men is to submit this day to the Lord's plan for their lives, knowing obedience is always better than sacrifice.

Just As I Am
Dr. Robert Martin

Just as I am, though tossed about
With many a conflict, many a doubt;
Fighting's within and fears without…

In 1972, I laid in my bedroom furious at my stepfather (QZ) and disheartened by my biological father (Harold). Fatherhood was not working so well in my life. Harold initially provided an infrequent presence that faded as I grew older. QZ married mom (Ellie V) when I was ten. He provided financial stability and disrupted our quiet routine with loud, harsh talk.

Each man left me empty and emotionally abandoned. I felt haunted by Harold's absence and misread, misinterpreted, and misunderstood by QZ. Truly, neither man nor I understood how their acts of fatherhood would affect the person – man, husband, father - I would later become.

That night in my bedroom at 16 years old, is the first time I distinctly remembered

thinking about becoming an adult. More specifically, I pondered my uncertainty regarding fatherhood. That night, I made an oath to myself and to my unborn children. With the exception of death or mental illness, I pledged not to subject them to what I was enduring. I would never leave them!

This introduction bookends a span of 40 years not mentioning an incredible mom, loving uncles, aunts and grandparents, influential church members and dedicated teachers. Reflecting back, it is evident I had support, guidance and mentoring along this journey. The nitty-gritty work happened while building a life with Kim, my wife and partner. We faced the trials and tribulations of raising our sons with the values of exposure, enhancement and enrichment.

At the time of this writing, our sons are 34 and 29 years old. As I reflect on their growing years, the one word that guided my parenting philosophy was 'intentionality.' The best decision I made was convincing my wife to marry me. Together, we created a warm and nurturing home.

We attended high school together and married after college. One area where we rarely had disagreements was our family. On one of our earlier dates, she described the type of family-life she aspired to develop, and I knew immediately she was the woman with whom I wanted to share my life. Our values were in sync. Her support has given me the space to find my path and journey in my desire to be an effective father.

After our oldest son was born, I decided on a fatherhood course of action that involved two deliberate actions:

1. modeling my actions after my mom
2. closely observing my maternal uncles, men from church and positive examples in society.

These men were always interested in my pursuits and supported me throughout their lives. One uncle moved in with me and Ellie V when Harold moved out. Another uncle supported his wife quitting her job to allow her the time to help babysit me while Ellie V completed Michigan teaching certification requirements. Church families included me in activities and allowed me to 'tag along.' This allowed me to witness firsthand how healthy families interacted and communicated.

Family time remained a priority for Kim and me during our boys' growing years. As educators, we used our summers for family vacations. We purchased a used travel-trailer and visited many of the national parks and major cities. We have memories of listening to howling wolves in Yellowstone Park, watching the sunset over the Grand Canyon and listening to the ocean waves lap against the shore in San Diego. Camping was a low-cost method of exposing our sons to many of the cultural icons in our society. During their adolescence, we traveled throughout Canada and Western Europe. It was important for them to fully participate in future adult conversations in various social situations. Intuitively, I was intentionally building their social-capital.

We felt it vital for them to be well-rounded individuals. Education was important. We closely monitored their academic progress and attended concerts, meetings and Parent-Teacher Conferences. They participated in Little

League, Soccer, Choir and school sports. I did not expect my wife to be the chauffeur and I tried to attend as many events as my work would allow.

I did not apply for administrative positions until they were older. I completed my Master's degree two months before our oldest was born and didn't begin my doctorate until our youngest was a senior in high school. I chose to make their well-being a priority.

I'm not perfect, but I am committed to be the best husband and father possible. When the boys were in their early elementary years, I developed an accountability friendship with another man from church. He and I met monthly to discuss challenges and specifically pray for me to develop 'intentional gentleness' with my sons. I felt that I argued too much and did not want them to perceive me as being too harsh. The last thing in the world I wanted was to take on the same negative characteristics I attributed to QZ!

Faith continues to be a foundational anchor in our lives. We worshipped together as a family, attended Christian camp, Youth-Group activities, and church-sponsored Mission Trips to Russia and Brazil. Our sons traveled to Switzerland and Guatemala as temporary missionaries without us. They remain on their personal faith journey as adults.

I wholeheartedly believe every son deserves his father or a father-figure. Our home has run much smoother due to the complementary gifts and skills Kim and I contribute. I must give credit to the extraordinary women who nurtured, guided, encouraged and pushed me through the years. At one point in my mid-twenties, I decided to just follow the role-model from EllieV: a faithful, resilient, gregarious and kind-hearted individual. It felt comfortable to use her attributes because I admired her so much.

One day, while preparing for work in 2012, I was shaving in the bathroom. My thoughts drifted to our oldest son completing his master's degree in Business and our youngest son's recent graduation from college. Something dawned on me at that time. Despite growing up the first ten years of my life with a single mom in inner-city Detroit and being Black. Despite struggling with an identity crisis around my unique 'nerdness.' Despite extreme insecurity around the type of husband and father, I might become. Despite all of this, it happened! I honored my oath to myself and kept my commitment to my sons. I stayed. *"Just as I am…"*

Tears.

Blessed To Be A Blessing
Marty Bulger

It is true that fatherhood is the most important role for a young person, a child, because children are validated by their dads. As I grew up in the city of Detroit, I learned that life as a young man would be challenging with winds, turns, and twists throughout. The events that I experienced growing up are the exact same experiences that I used to help my own children. That high level of involvement and engagement has given me the opportunity to use what I learned from my father and I cherish what I received from him. I have been able to impart those high qualities of fatherhood because of what I learned as a child.

Both of my parents have given me the strength, endurance, and ability to do the same for my four children. My mother taught me how to love, and my father taught me that hard work is love from a father's perspective. It behooves me to be a hard-working father as an example of fatherhood at its best. As a child, I woke up early in the morning to see my mother prepare breakfast and lunch for my father before he headed out to work. So now, all my children are diligent concerning their school and work activities. They have this mindset because they saw me get up early and get to work.

Now I am the example that I saw first in my father. My mother, with her hand on the Bible, and her heart steeped in its principles, taught me that I should read the Word of God daily and start my day off in prayer. So now, I expect all four of my children to read their Bible, and to get on their knees and pray before they start their day. These fundamental practices continue to yield results beyond any thought or dream. These practices are legacy moves to be cherished and reapplied generation after generation after generation.

My portrait of fatherhood lies in the understanding that **J** **O** **Y** is in honoring and serving **J**esus, **O**thers, and **Y**ourself, in that order. The circumstances of my childhood would not allow me to be in the position that I am, doing the things that I do, impacting the lives that I engage without these fundamental principles. I use them with my family, students, staff, parents, and community partners. We are able to touch lives because we first touch God at the start of our day. The Lord God Almighty is in control and we use His Word to guide and order our steps.

This recipe for success can only yield positive results when your heart and mind are open. Fatherhood is the first form of leadership, and leadership must have a set of principles that are tried and tested. The Bible says, "With God all things are possible." This scripture from Philippians four verse 13 suggests that we are able to do more because we recognize where our help comes from and how to apply it every day.

I love my four and many more, as my profession as an educator requires me to do. I love my four children. I love more, because the Word of God says that we are to love God and to love our neighbor as ourselves. Love looks differently to different people, but it looks the same to Almighty God. Fatherhood is a choice and this choice requires the ultimate commitment to obedience and sacrifice. Every day, like Mother's Day is Father's Day. We must embrace our roles as dads, and continue to be the example for our children.

To all of the fathers who have the opportunity to read the words that are written in this book, I say full steam ahead. Use every opportunity to bless your children. Use every occurrence of engagement with young people to be an example of the father that they long for so deeply. Understand and know that God's calling on your life is to be like Him in the lives of others. Let your courage be used to encourage, let your grace much more abound, let your mercy yield to love, and let your light so shine that men will see your good works. Dads, we must leave a legacy of love for our children that will cause God to say, "well done good and faithful servant".

A Statement on Friendship to Sons
Dathon O'Banion

"Well children //shan't call you kids//" in the words of Paul Lawrence Dunbar… Life can be boiled down to a *"crust of bread and a corner to sleep in"*.

Generally regarded as those individuals that you share direct bloodline through common ancestry family are the people that **should** help, love, and nurture you in all instances. According to the book of **Proverbs 18: 24,** "A man that hath friends must shew himself friendly: and there is a friend that sticketh closer than a brother." As a father, that is my first obligation. I will be your friend too in time. Friends are the ones that **will** help without the expectation of something in return. In this case, a friend is a surrogate family member. A friend perhaps surpasses the relationship you may have with family members who are not rooted in the true family spirit. It should be born in mind the flaw in the concept of family. Inevitable is the realization that "all" or even most family members will not be friends in the good or expected sense of the word.

Nurture friendships and don't ever betray the trust of a friend. This is a virtue of real manhood, son. If you feel that the friendship is not developing the way you think it should, (i.e. fostering a greater sense of mutual trust), you may have to re-evaluate that "friendship". Once, maybe twice, but never a third time! At that point, they have demonstrated they are not truly friendly, but only self-serving. I'm not saying that a friend will be without annoyances, faults, imperfections that will sometimes vex you.

To have a friend is to have one of the sweetest gifts that life can bring. A friend remembers us when we have forgotten ourselves or neglected ourselves. He takes loving heed of our health, our work, our plans, and our aims. He may praise us and we are not embarrassed. He may rebuke us and we are not angered. It takes a great soul to be a true friend. There are several virtues of a friend which you may learn as you experience the nuances of friendship. I, as a human being, simply say, "Be a friend." For me, as you know, "friendship is essential to the soul." A friend remembers us when we have forgotten ourselves or neglected ourselves.

Which brings me to your siblings; whereas you can always pick your friends, you cannot pick your family. Siblings and families that are smart should pool resources and not have "better than" or jealous rivalries within families or extended families. What I'm instructing of you, children, is to pool resources so that everyone benefits. This is a lifetime undertaking. So, if your brother or sister has children that need assistance going to college, everyone in the family should pull together without prejudice or notions of success to contribute to the success of the sibling's offspring. Share with each other in business ventures that can benefit each of you together. After all, you are flesh of my flesh and this is what your father wants. In other words, don't be selfish. If one sees an opportunity, share the same with your siblings so that all may have a right of refusal. Don't allow your siblings to be oblivious to the opportunity, all while the same opportunity has been extended to friends and acquaintances. Be a Brother and a friend.

007 (A Lesson in Life)
Richard T. Benson, Sr.

My two sons were visiting me for the summer. As the non-custodial parent, I was already at a disadvantage. At least that was the thought in my mind at the time. Their mom was on the west coast in Los Angeles, and I was on the East coast in New York City. This was definitely not a problem that Cliff and Claire Huxtable would face on, "The Cosby Show". But, this was my life. I had to make it work.

They were staying with me for about 3 months. As a single man of color living in Harlem, my goal was to occupy their time down to the last millisecond. Between summer classes at a private school in Queens, vacation bible school at a local church, review classes for the SAT, and long jogs or walks in the evenings, I pretty much had them active from dawn till dusk. Thank God, they were good kids that followed directions most of the time. That made it much easier.

Although I was really enjoying them, that schedule and pace were tiring the hell out of me. I had to make sure they were up, dressed, and out the door on time. I cooked breakfast, planned their lunch and had some form of dinner on the table every night. No captain peanut butter crunch cereal nights, like I often had when they were not with me. I could only imagine what their mom had to face.

After getting them out the door, I had to jump in the shower, throw on my clothes, catch the subway to West 110th street, walk 6 blocks to the medical center, take care of my patients, and attend departmental meetings occasionally. By the end of the day, my ass was beat.

Those things notwithstanding, the summer was going fairly well despite a few fist fights I had to break up between the boys; several meals with "extra-crispy" chicken; multiple cans of overcooked ravioli; broken furniture, and discolored clothes. We were all making due. The closeness of my one bedroom apartment on the ground level of the huge brownstone on Convent Avenue, made it difficult for any of us to have much private space. But, I guess tight space is a given living in Harlem.

We definitely had some passionate conversations. Those long jogs in Central Park, Riverbank Park or through the city were the best way for each of us to work off steam and get rid of extra energy. Jogging and going to church whenever possible, kept us spiritually tuned, mentally connected, and out of jail.

It was the last week of their vacation, so I took off work to do some sightseeing with them. We went to Time Square; saw "The Lion King"; The Statue of Liberty; and the world-famous Apollo theater. Boy did we have fun. Despite the toll all the entrance fees, food, souvenirs, and tickets had on my wallet, I was still determined to make sure they enjoyed the end of their summer vacation. I wanted them to have a summer they would remember for the rest of their lives. The irony of that thought was prophetic.

The day before they were to leave, I decided to take them to Coney Island. I have always loved amusement parks. The rides, the cotton candy, the sounds, the smells, the games, I wanted them to experience them all New York City style. Although we were all tired, we set out on that long subway ride from Harlem to Coney Island. For a brief instance, all I could think about was the movie, "The Warriors", when the triumphant gang made that long voyage from The Bronx to Coney Island, despite all the outside negative influences and obstacles. But, they made it. I smiled to myself knowing that the reference would be lost on my boys because of their age. In fact, we are "The Warriors", black men navigating this maze called life.

Using a smooth covert technique perfected over my time living in New York, I discretely pulled my wallet out and checked how much cash I had in it. I counted the twenty dollar bills. I had $300.00. That should be enough to get some Nathan hot dogs, a soda, popcorn or cotton candy, and a couple of rides. We were set.

As soon as we exited the subway, we were saturated by the intoxicating smells, the sounds, the people, and the excitement. It was a lot to take in, and I tried to imbibe it all. As we walked around, my eyes darted from side to side watching the people and my sons, thinking how much I wanted a hot dog.

Out of nowhere, over all the commotion, I heard a guy from one of the booths yell out, "Hey man, you feeling lucky today? Why don't you come try your hand at this? Win something for your boys". I looked in his direction. He was standing behind one of those wooden, rectangular, carnival booths. Although his facial features escape me now, he looked Italian, Greek, Hispanic or some mix of the three and had a slick New York accent.

The booth was scattered with these large and small stuffed animals hanging from the ceiling. In the back I noticed this large, brown and tan, stuffed dog with big floppy ears sitting on the ground. I thought to myself, "That must be about four feet tall. That would be cool to give to my boys".

I asked the guy, "So, what do I have to do to win that".

He said, "All you have to do is knock down these 10 pins 10 times and you win".

I thought to myself, "I could do that. I have pretty good aim. But, I hate gambling". I hesitated for a moment, then decided, "Why not try it?"

My boys were still looking around, taking in the sites. I told my older son, "Why don't you go get some hot dogs, then come back here". I gave him $20.00. I had $280.00 left.

I asked the guy behind the booth, "so how much does it cost"?

He said, "It's $1.00. But the price doubles every time you miss".

I thought to myself, "Ten tries. That's about $10 dollars, $20 dollars max. That's not that bad".

So, I said, "Ok that's cool. Let me try".

I gave him $1 dollar and looked at the 10 pens on the thick, flat table in front of me. They looked like bowling pins on a billiard's table, but slightly smaller. I got down to eye level with the table, pulled together all the physics principles I could think of at the time, blew some warm air in my hands, and rubbed them together. Then I skillfully rolled the ball down the table as precisely as I could. I knocked over all the pins. Those pins went flying to the side rails like they had been hit by a demolition ball.

I started smiling to myself and thought, "Yeah, I got this". My confidence was high. I wished my boys had been there to see it. I looked over and saw them buying their hot dogs. So, I continued.

I turned to the guy in the both and said, "Rack 'em up. I'm going for it." I gave him another dollar. I blew in my hands and sent the ball flying down the table. The crash of all the pins against the side rails had me grinning from ear to ear. I said, "Rack 'em up again. I'm going all the way". I repeated this action 5 times straight. That was $5.00 so far.

The dude behind the booth said, "You got this my brother. Let me rack 'em up for you". The arrogance in his voice was lost on me at the time. On the sixth try, I threw the ball down the table just like the previous 5 times, but this time there were two pins still standing. The guy behind the booth said, "Oh my brother you got this. Try again. That's $10 dollars".

I said, "What, what are you talking about. Ten dollars? That's robbery man."

He said, "You got this my brother".

I thought to myself, "Ok, that will be about $20.00 that's not bad. I went this far. I might as well continue. I bent down, looked at the table and blew in my hands. Right as I was throwing the ball my sons came back and said, "Dad, we're ready to go. We're tired". Just as they were speaking, the ball rolled out of my hand and hit the side rail. I had missed all of the pins. My ears felt like they were red with steam exiting the openings.

The guy says, "Why don't you try again my brother. You can do this. That's $20.00".

I yelled at my sons, "Wait a minute. I'm trying to win this damn dog. Give me a minute". I gave the man $20.00 with a frown on my face. I threw the ball down the table. This time there were still 3 pins standing. I thought to myself. Ok, now I can't stop. This dude is not getting over on me. I'm going to win this dog tonight. This shit was starting to get personal.

The dude says in a highly confident voice, "You got this my brother. That's $40.00".

I thought, to myself, "This is madness". But I couldn't stop. I gave the guy $40.00. I threw the ball down the table. This time, all the pins flew to the side of the table. My dwindling confidence nudged slightly in the positive direction. I felt sweat on my back causing my tee shirt to stick.

He said, "You got this my brother. Only 4 more tries. Give me another $40.00".

I thought to myself, "This is bullshit crazy. But, I can't lose now. This guy is not getting over on me, and I can't lose in front of my boys". So, I gave the guy another $40.00.

From that point on, all the subsequent events of that night were surreal. It was like an out of body experience for me. Maybe I was possessed or temporarily insane. I don't know. It's all a blur in my mind. But, after multiple more tries and one trip to a local ATM machine, before I knew it, I had raked out $700.00.

My sons were looking at me with frustrated eyes, "Dad we're tired. Can we go? We're ready to go".

The guy behind the booth was looking at me with a smirk on his face, "You want to try again".

I wanted to punch him in the face. But, I thought to myself, "This shit is crazy. I know this table must be rigged some kinda way".

Fighting hard to hold back the tears wailing up in my eyes, I cleared my throat and said, "Man I've given you $700.0. I think your table is rigged. You can at least give me that big dog back there. It's the least you can do after taking all of my money.

I glared at the guy behind the booth with a scowl, trying to hide my embarrassment. He arrogantly glanced at me and my sons, but eventually gave me the dog. I said, "Thank you" under my breath.

As I turned and walked away with my Pyrrhic victory, holding the large stuffed dog in one arm, and grasping the little one's hand with my free one, I used the dog's floppy ear to wipe the tears of anger and frustration from the corners of my eyes.

On the long train ride back, I told my boys, don't you dare tell anybody about this. This is our secret. We're going to call this dog "007", like the famous British spy. When we got home, I tucked them in on my sofa bed after they said their prayers. I then went into my bedroom and thought to myself, "What the hell was I thinking"? And, "I didn't get my damn hot dog".

The next morning, I took them to the airport and realized the dog was too big for them to take on the plane. It was the size of a small person. So, I kept the dog. To this day, I still keep "007" in my home.

My two main lessons from that experience:

> (1) Your family will love you despite your failures, losses, and faults. My sons didn't have time to pout with me. Life continued;

> (2) You shouldn't get so focused on your current circumstances and surroundings, that you don't realize the bigger picture. In other words, don't miss the forest for the trees.

I continue to remind myself and my sons these lessons even to this day.

One Hundred Words on Fatherhood
Gregory Anthony Montgomery II

I read somewhere that it is easier to build strong children then to repair broken men. Looking back on the past twenty years of raising two sons Khalid M and Malik M with the help of their beautiful mother Janeene M, I wanted to let future generations know what I learned. I will just elaborate on the top three things I learned.

Lesson One - Fear is not an option. A father cannot show fear. He must stand as a torchlight for his family. He must lead in a positive and fair manner without being overly aggressive.

Lesson Two - Be consistent and set the example. A father must show consistency. My sons could set their watches on me. They knew I would be where I said I was going to be when I was going be there and that was a comfort to them.

Lesson Three - It's always cheaper to keep her. When you find a good woman, you treat her right and you work it out. We need to build our families and show stability that gives our children and grandchildren a legacy they can build on.

These are just a few of the things I learned. Life is not perfect. There is no aha moment, but it is sweet and it is a gift. To my sons, be brave. Live proud and free. Never forget where you came from and always have a clear plan for where you are going. I love you...

Blessed Fatherhood
Reggie Dokes

When me and my wife got the news that we were expecting our first child, I was nervous. I think this is the norm for most expecting parents. Immediately you have those thoughts like, *"Am I ready for this?"*, or *"Will I be a good parent to this child?"* Finally, my nervousness subsided, and I realized that I had a great foundation; my parents. Unlike most young people today, I had both parents in the home. Needless to say, I was blessed. I had that mother growing up in Detroit, who showed me how important it was for me to work smart and speak up for the things I wanted. I had that mother growing up who showed me that how you present yourself, can either make you or break you. I had that mother growing up who showed me if you want certain things to happen in your life, sometimes you are going to have to fight for them. I certainly cannot forget my father. Here was a man who taught me about manhood. My father showed me the importance of being humble and selfless. He taught me that you could cry and still be a man. He taught me that you should never forget your roots. My father taught me that if you want a life of blessings, then give back or pay it forward. Lastly, my father taught me growing up that perseverance is necessary in the face of adversity. I was truly blessed to have my parents as a foundation.

So, in retrospect, I feel blessed that I was shown and given a great foundation, thanks to loving parents. Without question, my foundation has allowed me the opportunity to raise two great teenagers. Being a parent so far has taught me many things. As a parent, you sometimes have to let go and let life be their teacher. As a parent sometimes, you need to just listen and not always come up with a remedy. As a parent, sometimes you need to show your children that you walk what you teach them on a daily basis. As a parent, sometimes you need to admit that you were wrong. As a parent, sometimes you need to say, "*I messed up.*" As a parent, sometimes, you need to show up. As a parent, sometimes you have to put your needs aside for the betterment of your children. As a parent, sometimes you have to trust that what you put in them, will guide them and remain in their spirit to keep them on task. We can all agree that being a parent is not easy. We can all agree that you may get weary, but you cannot faint. We can all agree that parenting is not a journey to take lightly. We can all agree that good parenting should come from a good place. That place includes wanting to see our children succeed and see them have better experiences than we did. Remember, being a parent is a blessing and that is how I see it. Truth!

Fatherhood
"A Sacred Responsibility"
Rev. Dr. Gary A. Williams

Being involved in my son's birth was the most overwhelming, frightful and impressionable event I have experienced in fatherhood. It was being there that made being a father a reality. As life entered my hand and I cut my son's umbilical cord, it hit me hard that I was responsible for this new life and responsible to and for my wife.

I was frozen with anxiety, flooded with joy and I had a fear about the future. It hit me that this new little boy, who would be named after me would be looking to me for sustenance and guidance. It would be my job to teach, train, protect and provide for him. What a Blessing, what a responsibility! It would be my job to guide him and be to him what my dad was to me. It would be my job to be to him what my five older brothers were to their son(s) and daughters.

I saw sacrifice without complaint. Leadership without credit. I would have to be a leader, guide, friend and trainer. I would have to be a "good" example. I emphasize good because no matter what, I would be an example, so I was determined to be a good father.

I changed diapers and took the morning shift of feeding him. I kept him when his mom was otherwise engaged.

Notice I said, "*kept him*" not babysat. How can a father babysit his own child? Thus, I spent time with him, holding and hugging him, nurturing and caring for him. I bathed and dressed him. I was present with him. I told him I love him and I showed him the same.

I prayed over him, and I taught him how to pray, as my father had taught me to pray,

> Now I lay me down to sleep
> > I pray the Lord my Soul to Keep
> > If I should die
> > Before I wake
> > I pray the Lord
> > My Soul to Keep

I taught him there is a power greater than himself. I taught him he is great. The expectation of greatness was shared covertly and overtly. I thought it important to lead by example, so I made it a point to read to him and in front of him. I taught him to take a book with him wherever he went. A book of his choice, as he traveled and waited, he had a book to capture his attention and occupy his time. He was encouraged to choose his own book and began his own library. He was seduced into taking responsibility for his own education. These are the practices my wife and I agreed upon and put into practice. We worked together as a team.

Be informed that I have three sons by their mother to whom I am married. I say him but it is all three to whom I led this example and instilled the values and character traits. I sought to treat each son as an individual with unique gifts and talents. I wanted to pull out the best in them and to accentuate the positive. My goal was to work with their mother and my wife to give them the best opportunities possible for them to gain knowledge and experience. We took vacations together. My wife and I took vacations apart from our sons, demonstrating the necessity to be in good relationship with one's wife. A good father loves his wife, the mother of his children. A good father works with his wife to raise their children. A good father knows when to stand firm and when to compromise.

As a father, it is important to model intellect and brawn. It is important to use one's mind as well as one's hands. It is important to be thrifty, to plan and to think before one acts. Yes, it is important to have a plan. Yet one needs to be forgiving and resilient and to admit when one has made a mistake.

As a father, it is important to have a foundation. Mine is Biblical. I believe in God's Love. A few of my favorite scriptures are:

> Before I formed thee in the belly I knew thee; and before thou camest forth out of the womb I

sanctified thee, and I ordained thee a prophet unto the nations. **Jeremiah 1:5**

Then I heard the voice of the LORD saying, "Whom shall I send? And who will go for us?" And I said, "Here am I. Send me!" **Isaiah 6:8**

Therefore, shall a man leave his father and his mother, and shall cleave unto his wife: and they shall be one flesh. **Genesis 2:24**

For God so Loved the world that he gave his only begotten Son **John 3:16**

Whoever does not love does not know God, because God is love **I John 4:8**.

And ye shall know the truth, and the truth shall make you free **John 8:32**.

"I can do all things through Christ which strengtheneth

me." **Philippians 4:13**

And we know that all things work together for good to them that love God, to them who are the called according to his purpose. **Romans 8:28**

It is important to have a song. As a Prophet, one who speaks the truth and seeks to live the truth, my favorite song is Blessed Assurance. It is important to know your purpose. I believe my purpose is to serve my God. It is important to have a least one sermon.

This means taking care of my family, which starts with taking care of my wife. She is, "Bone of my bone, flesh of my flesh." It ends with taking care of my sons, my responsibilities. As I was present at literal birth. I have been present at many other special days such as reading days, recitals, promotion ceremonies, graduations, practices, piano lessons, tutoring sessions, and concerts. I sought to model the scripture in my thoughts, behavior and actions, and thus by practice transfer my values to my son. It is one thing to preach, it is another to do.

For a father, it is important to take to, drop off, participate with, and show your personality. It is important to be human and emotional. It is important to learn and ask questions and seek knowledge. It is important to cry, and then get up and fix one's mind on solving the problem at hand or facing the challenge that lies ahead.

I recently, asked my sons individually, what did I teach you?

> Son #1 said, "Self-Sufficiency."

> Son # 2 said, "Family first, work ethic, not to take crap from anyone."

>> Son # 3 said, "I learned how to work with my hands, have a side hustle, think for myself, be family oriented, read books, play an instrument, say what you mean, don't settle."

"Train Up a child in the way he should go, and when he is old, he will not depart." Proverbs 22:6 This was my wife's summation of the responsibility of fatherhood (a good father seeks the advice of his wife).

Often when I preach a man's funeral, I share that the greatest gift a man can give to his son is his faith. It is my hope that my son's see my faithfulness. My faithfulness to their mother, to them and to the community and world in which we live. I pray that the best sermon I preach, is the one I live! In doing so, I live fatherhood for my sons to experience and absorb and ultimately exhibit. I hope and pray they will pass on fatherhood to their children as did their grandfather and his father before him.

Real Fathers
Dr. Omari Daniel

Of course, not all men can be called fathers, but did you know not all fathers know how to be real fathers? The fraternity of fatherhood operates with the unwritten rules, the hidden culture, the subtext that most humans do not see. These rules separate deadbeats from dads and fathers from real fathers. A quick glance at a few examples will help illustrate these distinctions.

When given the choice to spend meaningful time with a child, bad men opt out and earn the label absentee fathers. Many men opt in, but not all are truly deserving to be inducted into the fraternity called fatherhood. For example, many men have taken their child fishing. But if that is all they did, they should simply be labeled a dad. A father takes his child fishing, but also makes sure there were adequate snacks, equipment, bug spray, and chances to catch a fish. But to be inducted into the fraternity of fatherhood, a man must do so much more. Members of the fatherhood know that fishing is just an excuse to have meaningful conversations with your child. We know that fishing is just a vehicle to listen to, understand, teach, and bond with your child. We know that if you ever caught the biggest fish in your life, your love and lack of false pride will cause you to give your rod to your child, so he can get the credit for the catch. We know even if they lose the fish, they are told they can never lose a father's love. We know that forming this bond makes you the person they come to for advice and help, instead of the person they avoid or never bother to consider consulting when they are in need.

When it comes to co-parenting, bad men opt out and let the momma raise the child. Dads are present and think that saying *"listen to your mother"* is somehow enough support and guidance. Fathers participate and partner with mothers to raise a child and give excellent feedback, support, and appropriate discipline. However, the members of the fraternity called fatherhood know much more. We never allow a child for one minute to believe that the mom is anything but an equal partner. They understand that if their children think the father is the only one in charge, they will grow up thinking women are subservient. Or, in the case of female children, they run the risk of becoming subservient women. We know that raising a child requires giving up your entire life to them. So, your successes and failures can be scrutinized to benefit your child. We also know that we never take out our work frustrations on our kids. We understand that our challenges at work do not put a belt or whip in our hands to be used against our children. We also know that no matter what a child does, our love is never withheld. While the world may withhold its love from our children because they may be gay, Black in America or because they made a mistake, as fathers, we never can abandon them.

Finally, members of the fraternity of fatherhood do not subscribe to stereotypes about men that could cripple our children. We cry because we are human, and we do not teach young boys to be heartless creatures. Because we respect all women, our sons can imitate us, and our daughters can know what to anticipate and never settle for less. We give our children the truth always, so they don't grow up thinking all men are liars. We never tell a child it is my way or the highway. Instead, we build bridges together and help make a new way. We take care of our health, so that we can stay in our children's' lives longer. And one day, we do the hardest thing in the world. We let our children grow up and accept them as our peers and equals. And, we can learn from them too.

The Least….
Kevin Morgan

Wayne Duerson was amazed that such ordinary words could carry so many negative emotions. Even at the age of 41, he still struggled to accept the reality that it really wasn't the words, but the person who spoke them that stung him. The mother of his three children, all boys, hurled those words in his direction. *"The least you can do is buy the suit."* Simple words that summarized the highs and lows of their relationship. Was the anger betrayed by the tone behind her words because he never married her? Or was the anguish due to the fact he was hovering on the outside of their lives?

He looked at the dark blue suit with the faint grey pin stripes. The helpful lady at the thrift store who asked him the right questions about height and weight gushed that the suit would be perfect for any occasion. As he balanced the need to buy a suit against the fear of not being able to afford it, he inwardly whined that there was no way he could face his boys' mother without that suit in his hands. Wayne silently wondered why the sales lady's words to him were much more benign than the not so subtle hurtful words from the mother of his sons. How can the words of a stranger be more comforting than the words that were launched at him from the mouth of the woman he once loved?

It's just a suit, he mumbled to himself. But as the words from his non-wife echoed in his heart, he knew that suit carried more meaning than he cared to admit. Those words accused him. Without spelling it out, she expressed her disappointment and frustration in him. Her slightly squinted eyes that flashed so much anger at him backed up the charge that she viewed him as less of a man and a poor excuse for a father. He mindlessly smoothed out the wrinkles deeply embedded in the slightly used suit. His shoulders slumped under the weight of being reduced to the titles of a sperm donor and a not so present father.

"The least you can do…." Wayne feared that his boys' mother had set the bar so low that he was descending to her trite expectations. Momentarily turning away from the suit, he tried to pinpoint exactly when he chose the path of least resistance to becoming an absentee father? Was it the time he didn't show up at his oldest son's little league baseball game? Was it during one of the many weekends he broke his promise to swing by their house to see his boys? Maybe it was the birthday cards never sent or the father to son discussions he never initiated. Somewhere in his life, he allowed his least effort to become his best effort at being a dad.

When his wife first spoke those words about the suit, he just stood there waiting for her to say more. During that tense and uncomfortable silence, he found it hard to look directly in her eyes. The defiant way she tilted her head to the left and squared her shoulders, he knew that attitude behind her words packed more punch than anything else she might have wanted to say. No further instructions or accusations, just a declaration of the "*least*" he could do. It was almost as if she was daring him to be more or do more. Was this a dare or a plea? Was she opening the door to him stepping up and being the man she needed and the father the boys craved? Wayne slowly turned back to stare at the suit lying on his bed. He ashamedly admitted that he almost felt relieved when through her defiant silence, it became clear that his wife's focus was on the suit and not an invitation for him to step up as a father or a man.

After taking a deep breath, Wayne picked up the suit and headed towards the front door of his modest house. Once in the car, he pressed the ignition button and began to slowly back out of his driveway. He turned on the radio and hummed to himself as the song being played slowly faded away. After a few seconds of silence that reminded him of the awkward quietness he shared with his boys' mother earlier today, his ears prickled with the breaking news headline being broadcast throughout his car's sound system. *"Police spokesperson announces the investigation into the shooting death of suspected drug dealer, Wayne Duerson, Jr is ongoing. Although no gun was found at the scene of his shooting, the police insist they thought they saw the victim pointing a gun in their direction. Mr. Duerson, also known by his street name "WD2" is scheduled to be buried tomorrow."*

"*The least....*" Those two words from his boys' mother seemed to be reflected in the actions of the police since the shooting death of his son. The least the police did was investigate his now dead son's past. The least they did was run with the rumor that because his son was from a certain side of town, he most likely was selling drugs. The least they did was disregard the fact that Wayne Jr was a good student with a "B" average who was set to attend a local university to pursue an engineering degree. The least they did was ignore the past of the White police officer who shot his son five times.

Headed to the house of his boys' mother to deliver the suit for his murdered son, Wayne smirked at a tragic irony. Because of his failings as a father, his son was victimized by the least he did to be in his son's life. Because of the amount of least diligence of the police officer, his son was shot to death. Because of the least effort in investigation, his son's death would be ruled a legal shooting by the police.

Gripping the steering wheel as he trembled with a mixture of remorse and shame, Wayne vowed to break the cycle of the least that wreaked havoc for him as well as in the lives of his boys and their mother.

What's The Matter With White People?
Finally, I Believe I See
Kenneth M. Moore
Author's Note

I sat down to write the article you are about to read in the winter of 2016. That winter was certainly a volatile and contentious time in our national history. There was no indication even then, with cold sweeping across the nation both literally and figuratively, that the volatility of that time would pale in comparison to what we now face as this book goes to print in 2020.

The words and emotions expressed in the article to come are deeply personal and are, in my humble opinion, timeless. I literally found my face soaked in tears attempting to complete the writing of it. This introduction is not intended to alter, soften, or harden any of the values or beliefs expressed in the article. It is simply to clarify that history . . .herstory is ever evolving and that my feelings for individuals who may have taken a certain position in 2016 are not necessarily my feelings regarding those who make the same choice in 2020. I sincerely hope that you will take something of value, whether you find it thought provoking or view it solely as entertainment from my words and story to follow.

****

It is a question that's been asked time and again in recent years. It has been the subject of articles, bestselling books and endless personal discussion. I think I've arrived at an answer. It was a long and arduous journey to arrive at this place of understanding. The road to seeing white people was a twisted and mangled road. I'm not talking about the White Nationalists, marching in the streets, or the "Birther's", who believe that President Obama was secretly born in Kenya but rather I'm discussing the ones who shocked you and me in 2016. The people who we all know and even spend time with on occasion. They are the voters in places like Ohio, Michigan, Wisconsin, Pennsylvania, West Virginia and nationwide who turned the tide of the nation. Those are the people that I've come to recognize and maybe even understand a bit. Now, I said that the pathway to seeing these folks was long and convoluted, but ironically, I did not have to travel far. This journey led me to the most familiar of places. It took me home.

Can you see, at the top of the grassy hill, next to the church, there's a small, white, wood frame house . . . the one with the cement slab porch that runs the twenty-foot length of the front of the small dwelling. The one with the grey shingled roof overhanging the porch. Yes, it is the house that looks like something right out of an antebellum slavery scene. I would say that it is an old Victorian style house, but it is too small and cheaply made to have the honor of having a style attached to it. That is home, my home.

At the foot of that house lies eight or so feet of scattered plugs of grass and dusty brown and red Tennessee soil, that is our front yard. The big man with the broad NFL linebacker or heavy weight boxer like shoulders, do you see him? His copper brown skin and dark, medium length afro contrast nicely with the green polyester "leisure" suit he's wearing. The suit along with the wide collared polyester shirt and patent leather shoes suggests that it's the 1970s but it may be later in time as, like most poor men of his era, he's held on to that one suit just a little too long. The gold band around his left ring finger always seems a touch out of place on such large, strong, rough hands. They are hands that almost never look or come completely clean from the grease and grime of a hard, blue-collar life. Those hands are occasionally further decorated with the burn of a red-hot rivet or the molten metal welding shards, that tattoo his knuckles, fingers and palms regularly. They are a working man's hands and certainly not the type of hands that jewelry should adorn but rest assured that ring never comes off that third left finger. This is a man who is proud of his wife and two boys and even more proud that he can place a roof over their heads and food on the table. Do you see him?

You might recognize the look on my Dad's face today with his bright still youthful eyes and almost mischievous little boy grin. He hurries my mother and his two boys inside from the church lot after one of the rare times that Mama could get him across the street and into Sunday church service with us. The mischievous smile is because he knows he's cutting short Mama's gossip time with the other ladies from the church so that we can make it to our seats in front of our small, "floor model" television to watch first, the afternoon football game, then Marlon Perkins and his early evening nature show Mutual of Omaha. Can you envision that mountain of a man child? That man is my father.

In the morning, Pop is up before the sun rises, drinking a cup of scalding hot coffee that either he or my mother prepares. As he sips his coffee he laces up his work shoes. The shoes that my father wears to work are not wing tips, Bostonians or Stacey Adams. Pop pulls on heavy steel-toed boots that bear very similar burn marks to those on his hands. There are no suits, ties, slacks or pressed white shirts in Pop's work time wardrobe. Work clothes for my dad include only heavy, green or blue Dickey's and thick matching long-sleeve shirts with a sewn-on patch bearing his name and on the other side of his broad chest, the name of the enterprise for which he works. So many of us see a shirt like the one Pop wears and want to laugh just a little. We may even over emphasize the name, Joe or Frank or Troy, on his chest as we address these men, as if they should be just the slightest bit ashamed that their names are sewn onto their chests. We sometimes act as if those patches are there because they might otherwise forget the name, they've carried all of their lives. But like that not overly expensive gold band on his finger my father is proud to wear that shirt, name patch and all. That patch symbolizes the struggles of graduating from a segregated high school in a small-town Tennessee and of joining the military during war time as all, but the most privileged boys did at that time. The patch on my father's chest symbolizes his journey from the military back to that small town where he managed to convince the executives at the local power plant that he was worthy of their apprenticeship program to become a machinist. And that patch symbolizes the pride that he graduated from that apprenticeship and moved into what folks called a "good job" . . . a job that would allow him to pay at least the essential bills every month and buy the five or so outfits that my big brother and I would get annually for our "school clothes". Do you see him now? Can you envision a proud man just happy to be a decent provider for his family?

He's a good man. He's the type of man who takes his sons to every football, baseball and basketball practice. And when the many kids, whose fathers we never see, need rides to and from the practice field, Pop is the type of man who piles as many boys as will fit into his old, used car and delivers each one to their homes. It doesn't matter how far on the other side of town Pop must go; each boy gets delivered to his front door.

But this man is not a man without demons. They are the kind of demons brought on by the monotony of dragging oneself to the same job day after day, decade after decade knowing that this is likely the only life he'll ever know. Demons which are created over time; time that sees my father train younger, white workers only to watch them be named his boss soon thereafter. This is the darkness generated from the stress of years in which a broken bone at football practice for his son or a rise in the blood pressure of his elderly mother or father make paying even those essential monthly bills impossible. This darkness pushes him even further from being the family provider he wants to be so desperately. The demons of hopelessness urge him further into the darkness that allow him to take his thick leather belt to the backsides of his two sons, which everyone refers to as "such good boys", far more often than any of their small transgressions warrant. These are demons that turn the one or two beers after work of a young and idealistic man, to the five, six, seven or more daily beers of a forty-year-old man. They are the constant acts of a man that make a young boy wonder what must taste so good inside that whiskey bottle that his father pours it to the rim of those large drinking glasses so often. Those demons are even the occasional impetus for the bruises on the neck or across the check bones of a sobbing mother; the bruises conspicuously matching perfectly the right hand of a father growing further and further away from his growing sons and wife. Can you see the whole of this man? Can you see the darkness and the light?

It's been many years since he's pushed his young sons to a point nearing hatred for the demons and the man who bore them. Decades have now passed since a little boy proclaimed his Daddy could do anything and young sons would see the glow and pride in a young father's eyes, as he placed a few dollars in those little boys' hands. Those glowing young eyes have been replaced by the permanent jaundice yellow of a failing liver and heart. But that old man, full of demons, emerges from the dark and is called by his savior to come back to that small church across the street. He was a good man that so many of those little boys from the football fields saw as almost a surrogate for their absent fathers. He was also the man blessed with a stubborn wife who stood by him through the struggles, the pain and even the abuse. That same man emerges from the black of his life to become even better than anyone ever believed he could be. Still he can't get back those years that his demons stole from his children. No matter how hard he tries or how good he lives his life he must carry yet another weight on his now withering shoulders.

Do you know this man and his broken heart?

Whether it is the religious epiphany that changed this man or perhaps the need for absolution and a return of the admiration he once saw in the faces of little boys and a young wife, only Pop will ever know. But my father gained the inspiration and strength to return to the classroom at nearly sixty years of age, enrolling in college to study his newly found calling of Christian philosophy. The same pride that he showed in putting food on the table and providing for us for so many years pushes him to work all day, study all night and travel over two hours several days a week to pursue his dream. It is that same something inside a man that prompted my father to confess to me during a last phone conversation, as he lay in the hospital with a failing heart, "son, I'm just worried about my grades. . .I made the Dean's list and I just want to keep my grades up. I want you guys to be proud of me too". My father would be taken from us soon thereafter. Can you see the totality of a man's life? Do you recognize the tortured, difficulty he lived? Can you see the bravery and the triumph? It took decades of living life and gaining understanding for me, his son, to truly see all the dark and greatness that existed in my father.

My Father is no longer with us. I certainly don't presume to speak for him, but I suspect that he would want you to see the whole of who he was. And equally I believe that he would try to see the complete story of those men, like him, who worked day in and day out for decades in the grease and flying hot metal flecks of that power plant next to Pop. He would remember the names like Smitty and Fritz and Footsie. Pop would know how they all left that plant in the dimming light carrying thick metal lunch pails, insulated thermoses and their near broken bodies home to their families. My father would remember how his boys were welcomed in so many of their homes and on their farms. He would recount how a Saturday of bareback horse riding and catching crawdads in the creek with the blondest, blue eyed little boys and girls would take his little black children away from their inner-city lifestyles for just a moment. And my father would understand that these men were very much like him. They too just want to see their children's eyes light up as they place the small amounts of cash that they can spare into their kids' pockets. They would want to see the smile on her face when they muster enough money to help pay for a daughters inexpensive wedding. Those men also want to feel some sense of pride as they send just a few dollars for spending money to their child struggling through college working a night job and overloaded with student debt. Yes, my father's challenges were greater in many ways than some of those men, but Pop would on some level understand them. He would know that when the snake-oil salesman came to town selling dreams of bringing back their jobs and their only opportunity to feel like providers, fathers, and men, that they would be believers again in yet another dream deferred. Pop would understand that they would do almost anything to get that patch back on their chests that so many of us thought they should be ashamed of wearing. Pop would understand the lifting of the desperation that the words of that snake-oil salesman represents. He would know the allure of the pitch of the snake-oil salesman even if it was no more likely that his elixir would generate a cure than playing the lottery. Pop would recognize that his words, no matter how dishonest, represent a chance that some of his friends might have to take. Pop would say, "what's the matter with white people? Not much that's not wrong with you and me". I'm certainly not suggesting that my father would have agreed with their choices, as I'm sure he would not, but he would know those men. He would understand those men and he would see those men, those husbands, those fathers.

Can you see them too?

Stability
Rev. Levonia Belt

Generational relationships in the 40's and 50's were lacking stability. Lifestyles for African Americans in this period of time were more about individuality then family.

My mother at age 15 bore my oldest brother and two years later, my second brother at 17 in a separate family.

My father, after returning from World War II, had a lifestyle of a crooner. He would sing at many clubs in Philadelphia, PA. At 24, he fathered a daughter with a recent high school graduate. They never developed a family lifestyle. My father re-enlisted in the Navy and set up an allotment for his daughters' well-being.

Our family became a partial unit at my birth. We never became a full family unit until my fathers' death in 1969.

In the middle sixties, my father began the discussion of sex with me and my brothers. He explained that young ladies would present me opportunities and I would do well by walking away if possible.

I did my best.

One thing I professed, I would have two sons. After living well until age 27, I met the soon to be mother of my sons. We broke my cycle of no children before marriage. My wife came from a family of 10, a very stable family.

We raised our sons' in a Christian home. I taught the boys to respect their mother and everyone they met. I did not teach Santa Claus or the Easter bunny.

Wanting a blend of Father Knows Best, Donna Reed and the Cosby show, we wanted a stable family. In the mid eighties and being a first Black in corporate life, we did the best we could without the background and training. We used the Bible as our guide.

Traveling around the country, I personally made the effort to being present at home for dinner and for family time every Thursday. Worship service every Sunday. Striving for consistency, we were successful and happy.

Our sons had possessions that only a few families from our upbringing had.

Growing in the corporate world took me away from home more than I desired. Gone weeks at a time put a great strain on our family. I would miss countless events of my sons' life. I began to despise my lifestyle and felt the pressure from home.

After eighteen years as a family, we grew apart. The solace of a successful story started with an agreement of joint custody and the hope with support from mother and father and an entire family unit. The boys now mid teens and a high school graduate, embarked on a very well communicated life. Communication was well a prime example of success.

Everything that was done began and ended with fulfilling their desire. Communication was the sole emphasis for our stability.

After understanding my oldest sons desire to fly and not attend college, we set him on his course for life. Day in and day out, he would train. He did so well at the airport where his training took place, he gained employment and was around airplanes all day everyday. His success led him to a job flying for a company delivering bank notes across the country. This period gave him time to build up his flight time and he became an airline pilot for a major airline.

The communication and the stability to focus on our son's hope and dreams are a success. Now flying for over seventeen years, a homeowner and contemplating a family of his own, stability is real.

My second son wanted college and a goal to play college basketball. Our endeavor was focused on making this request come true. Once again, communication and stability were necessary to complete this task.

Turmoil the first year turns into success. After graduation, he played basketball overseas. Returning home, my son turned to his second goal. He wanted to be involved in investigative work. He returned to college and obtained a Master's degree in his field.

My second son is now employed in his desired career field with a family of his own.

The effort of many families is about stability.

Stability is the base for success. We all need to have our hopes and dreams built on a firm foundation. Everyone one desires to have a perfect family, lifestyle, children and career. All of us have the obligation to develop a legacy of success.

I've taught our sons that their life is built on a strong foundation. That focus on ones' own goals and not on past distractions or current blockades can deter them from their own successes.

The legacy that was started is their stability. I've found a number of men and women wanting to blame their past for the problems they've incurred in their present life. Your effort is to note that one's stability is life itself. You're breathing, you're stable, you woke up this morning and clothed in your right mind and you're stable.

Stability is who you want to be.

May I just add? Jesus was born to a virgin who never knew man. He was relocated on several occasions and had to deal with the love of His parents as stability. Everyone should find their own stability and strive for their own success.

Two Homes, One Heart
Carlos Jones

I became a father at the age of 32. I went through a lot of changes of heart when it came to wanting to have a child. There was a time that I didn't want children because I was afraid of failing as a father as my father did. Then when I thought I was ready for children, I did not want to raise someone else's children because of the bad experience I had being a step-child. As life would have it, my life went in directions I could not have planned. I am now the biological father of one daughter and the step-father of three more daughters. I am using the term "step father" here just as a point of clarification. I am a father, pure and simple.

My first wife and I married when we were both 29 years old and we did not rush into having children. When our daughter arrived three years later, life was good. All my fears about being a failure as a father subsided. I was committed from day one to being a great dad to my daughter. I had it all planned out- we would have the 2.5 kids, the house on the hill, and live happily ever after. Unfortunately, the happily ever after ended in a divorce and me living in another house before my daughter was four years old. At first, the separation was not that bad because my new residence was only around two miles away from my daughter. Being able to see her everyday helped ease the guilt and embarrassment of divorce.

Failing at marriage did not have to mean failing as a father.

My new life was built around being a great father to my daughter. Everything and everyone came second to her in my life. In my mind and in my heart, I was content on remaining a single father and just enjoy life watching my daughter grow up. Obviously, God had different plans for me because he sent a new woman into my life. I met a young widow with three young daughters of her own and she lived in another city. What started as a blind date turned into a long-term relationship that led to marriage three years later. After a lot of careful thought and consideration, I made the hard decision to move with my wife and her daughters to her city. I was no longer two miles away from my daughter. I was now 100 miles away and officially my worst nightmare- a weekend dad.

I was the child of divorce. My parents divorced when I was really young. My mother was remarried by the time I was 7 and my dad was remarried a few years later. My relationships with my mother's husband and my father were never great. I have to say that I was not physically abandoned by my father. My father was around and I spent a lot of time with his side of the family. But I never felt like I was a priority to him. I can count on one hand the school and other life events when my father was present. My dad had demons of his own to deal with and he let those demons keep him from being a father. Those demons prevented him from being the father that my brothers and me needed. My mother's husband never put forth a true effort to be a father figure to me. While my father was around and I lived in the house with my mother's husband, I truly felt as if I was a child of a single mother. My personal life experience led me to make two extremely anxiety filled and gut-wrenching decisions; move away from my daughter and to take on the responsibility of being the father figure to my wife's daughters.

While I was no longer close by proximity to my daughter, I was determined not to let that interfere with my relationship with her. Additionally, I had to work to earn the love and trust of my new daughters. I was determined not to let my life experience be the life experience my girls would remember. I made it my job to be as present as possible in the lives of all the girls. I can tell you that it was not an easy task, but it is a job that I took to heart. I was present at every game, school program, or other life event that I could be. It took a very serious situation to make me miss one of their events. It required a lot of organization, time management and partnership with my wife and ex-wife to make all of this possible. Thankfully, technology made being present even easier. I talk, text, or Facetime with my daughter every day. My biological daughter has never had to feel slighted or wonder if her dad would be there. My bonus daughters know that I love them and that they can count on me.

I have made a lot of mistakes and missteps in my life and I have gotten a lot of things wrong. But being a father is one of the things I try exceedingly hard at getting right. If that means driving an hour to spend 15 minutes at my daughter's honor roll program and then drive an hour back, then that's what I will do. I will tell all fathers, biological or not, do not let divorce or distance keep you away from what God called you to do. No excuse is ever good enough to stop you from being a presence in your child's life.

A Better Portion
Bruce Strouble

There is a song which was sung by the late great Luther Vandros, which I love performing whenever an opportunity presents itself. It is entitled, "Dance with My Father". Each time that I've had a chance to sing this song it has become my habit to dedicate it to all of us less than perfect fathers in the world. Now, in somewhat that same tradition I have written this next poem, and dedicated it to my sons, and all sons who will be fathers.

As a child

It was my father

Who symbolized strength to me

He was powerful and capable

And though he knew little

Of affection or adoration

I sorted through the quality

Of his offerings

Then etched what I thought best of him

Into my own character

Thus I came to understand

What he could not offer freely

Was not a failing in his humanity

But merely a portion

Not passed on to him by his father

I considered this many times

Over the years

And decided that I would offer

To my sons a better portion

That I would be a constant presence

Which rendered pride, affection

Adoration, communication

Where I have fallen short

I hope that they will not see it

As a failing in my humanity

But realize there was merely a portion

Which was not passed on to me

By my father

So my challenge to all here today

Who are, or will be fathers

Offer your sons, your children

A better portion

Offer them the best of who you are

The best of what you know
So that the best of your qualities can be etched
Into their characters
So that they, your children might have a chance
To build upon a solid foundation
Which will support and influence
Generations to come
I challenge all sons to exceed your fathers

You may follow the paths
Which they have taken
And see where they have marked the pitfalls
So that you might avoid them
Where they have spread their wings and soared
Spread your wings even further
Soar even higher
And where your fathers have fallen short
Get beyond it
And where they still lay beaten in the roads ways
With God's gentle grace step over them
So that one day you can reach back

And help them forward

Teaching future generations

An even greater lesson

Inevitably our lives are all about

The choices that we make

It is our responsibility to leave a legacy

Which reflects the quality of those choices

To truly offer a better portion

A father's challenge should

Consistently be

         EXCEED ME!!!

Developing the Father in You
Rev. James W. Gladden

One night about two weeks ago, I was sitting in my room observing my 4 year-old daughter play with her dolls. I watched how she took care of them, fed them, clothed them, and put them to bed. She even would have full blown conversations with them; telling them how much she loved them. At that point, something hit me. I realized that I never really thought about fatherhood until I became a father. That delayed realization hindered me from being the father that my children needed me to be. When I had my first son (who is now 16 years old), I did not know what I was doing. I was clueless about what to do with a child. I did not know how to spend time with him, how to play with him, or even how to talk to him. At times, I would be so baffled when I looked at him because I was so lost. There were times when while he was sitting on the floor and playing with his toys, he would look to me to join him. But I was so dumbfounded that I did not even know where to start. I was so confused about being a father, that I purchased a television and placed it in his room. That was my clumsy way of not dealing with being a father at all.

Instead of trying to come up with excuses about my poor fathering skills, I will just man up. I own the fact that I did not even try to become a good father at that time. When my second son was born (who is now 13 years old) much of the same behavior continued because I just did not know what to do. Because I was a terrible father at that time, it caused a strain on my marriage that almost caused me to lose my family altogether. But something happened to me that changed my life forever. God made it to where I had to deploy on consecutive tours to Iraq to teach me a lesson. When He sent me over there, He began to speak to me about fatherhood in ways that I had never been spoken to before. The first thing that God told me was that if I did not become a better father to my children, He would take them away from me and give them to someone else. That revelation brought me to my knees. Then God said that while it is important what I do with my children, it was more important they knew that I was there and that I was active in their lives. That Godly advice helped me to conclude that not knowing what to do was not an excuse for being a bad father. His words of guidance reminded me that what really mattered was the effort I put forth to be a really good father to my children. So, during those deployments, I made a point to call them regularly and spend time talking to them. I made a genuine effort to get to really know them. I wrote them letters and expressed how I really felt about them. I made a point to listen to their mother to see if they were behaving accordingly. I even sent them DVDs with me reading them bed time stories, so they could know that I would continue to behave in that manner upon my return. By doing those things, I realty developed a passion for fatherhood that made me a better man.

The two major things that I have learned to being a better father goes as follows:

1. Just because you have a child, does not mean that you are a father…

It literally takes time to develop into the father that you desire to be. That means if you have to seek out mentors who can assist you in becoming a father, then you must do what it takes to be who your children need you to be. There is a saying that more things are caught, the more they can be taught. So get around some men who you feel are exceptional fathers, and glean from the knowledge that they have acquired over time.

2. Spend 30-minutes to an hour a day giving your children undivided attention…

Contrary to popular belief, you really do not have to spend hours upon hours a day with your children. They just want to know that you will dedicate time with them, doing what they want to do; no matter what that is. Allow them to decide what they want to do, and participate in that activity. When I was first starting out as a father, one of my biggest issues with fatherhood was that I thought I had to spend large quantities of time with my kids. But I finally learned they just want us to show up, and often times that does not require much from us at all. My question to you is this: What do you want your legacy to be when it is all said and done? That legacy will only last as far as your seed takes it. We must spend that time imparting the wisdom that our children will need as they get older, and ultimately move on with their lives. We must also understand that parenting is a lifelong process, so we must always grow in this area. We must strive to be who our children need for us to be in whatever phase of their lives they are in. That will make the biggest difference in the world to them and to us. Do we have to be perfect fathers? The answer is no! But I do believe that we can be excellent fathers who show up for our children no matter the cost. In order to be an excellent father, and the dad that your children deserve, you must continue developing the father in you.

Fatherhood
Milton Jones

Being a father is one of the most rewarding challenges I will ever encounter in my life. There are many definitions of fatherhood. This is how I define fatherhood, a present male in the lives of his children who leads by example. He exhibits the following traits by being a: leader, priest, teacher and lover. A leader makes things happen by being an example, taking initiative, setting a course (*the road less traveled*). A priest is a man of God, modeling authentic worship for his children, leading family worship and encouraging his children to have private worship (*one-on-one time with God*). A teacher imparts knowledge, wisdom and builds character, giving your child a personal testimony. A lover gives a child what they need in order to become their best version of him or herself. There is a saying in education; fairness is not everyone getting the same, but everyone getting what they need to succeed. A father who is a leader, priest, teacher and lover fulfills his fatherly role by ensuring each of his children are properly prepared to reach their potentials.

Love is the key to everything. If you love your kids, show them by demonstrating your love through action. When I was a kid, my mom was the heartbeat of the family, but dad was our rock. My Dad played a critical role in the lives of me and my siblings, beyond providing money, clothes, and a roof over our heads. A picture comes to mind of a big, strong tree in the backyard. My dad was like an old oak tree that spreads its branches across the sky like open arms. He was a place that kids could run to in the morning to play near or hang around in for comfort.

My dad passed away in 2012, two days after my 31st birthday. It seems at least a few times a year, I understand or have a better understanding of lessons that my father taught. My father was by far the greatest man I knew. He was tough, firm and sometimes unrelenting. I didn't start to have a great appreciation for my dad until I went away to college. Now that I'm a father, I have a better understand of things my father did and why.

As a Father, I want to build that same sense of unshakable security? I want to be the Father who says to his kids, *"Come, come sit on my lap. What did you do today? Did you make a mistake? What did you learn?"* I want to build the same relationship with my kids that God has with each one of us. I want to be willing and ready to share a laugh, give a word of encouragement or wipe away a tear. The father can be stern, yes, but always in a loving way. Consequences and correction may come, but he never speaks out of condemnation. I want both of my daughters to feel safe and confident that I always have their best interests in mind.

Fatherhood is about being engaged with your kids and actively participating in their day-to-day lives. He spends time talking and playing with them and holding them when they need to be held. It's about always aiming to be present, not fleeing into a *"man cave"* or escaping to work. Those diversions are short, flighty things compared to your relationship with your kids. I strive to be a better father each and every day of my life.

A Father's Test of Faith: What Do You Say When God Says No?
Jerome S. Nesbitt

As a father, it was my primary responsibility to protect, provide and prepare my children for anything they would possibly encounter as they grew into productive citizens. This was especially true when it came to my son. I understood there were things I needed to share with my daughter from a man's perspective, but I knew certain lessons she would need to get from her mother. I took a different approach with my son Deuce. I knew I needed to teach and prepare him from the lenses of a Black man. I had to make sure he understood the importance of producing his best and that no one should ever outwork him. While this task was very important to me but vital to him, I felt my main priority was to keep him and the rest of my family out of harm's way.

We took extra precautions with our children when it came to activities outside of our home. When they asked to attend sleep overs, it took a very intense meeting of the minds before each discussion. When he was in Cub Scouts, we were in cub scouts. When he played organized basketball, I was his basketball coach. This not only gave me the satisfaction of teaching and a level of protection; it also gave us an opportunity to spend time together. We shared the same pregame meal and listened to the same pregame songs before every game. During that time, I shared with Deuce to pray with expectation, but what do you do when God tells you "no"?

We spent so much time protecting him from everything we thought could ever come his way. Who knew that the one thing we couldn't protect him from was the uninvited dreaded and deadly disease called cancer? In January of 2018, our lives changed forever. After a normal weekend spending time together, who would've known that later Sunday night he would be found non-coherent and would require immediate emergency assistance. We assumed it was a severe case of the flu, only to find out Deuce had a mass on the frontal lobe of his head and would require immediate surgery to have it removed. When the doctors told us the news, we immediately went into prayer posture and shared the news with Deuce. When I shared with him what needed to happen, his only response was, "Okay Dad". We prayed with him and off he went into surgery. Surgery went well and he bounced back to his normal self at a rate that was surprising to his doctors. We weren't surprised at all because we know the God we serve. The fact he was home with me in seven days watching the Super Bowl was amazing within itself.

Within months we got the news that the mass was a very aggressive form of cancer and the treatment plan needed to be equally aggressive. I never knew how strong and anchored in the faith my son was until that day when we shared the news with him. He responded in saying, "I'm good, God's got me". From that day on, God continued to move mountains, knock down barriers and show us favor that could only come from Him. His favor landed us in the care of some of the best physicians in the world at St. Jude Children's Hospital Memphis, TN. I was unsure of the acceptance process, but I can tell you God's process put us in contact with an angel at St. Jude. Within forty-eight hours, we were on a plane to Memphis to begin treatment. Once the treatment started, Deuce did great. All the symptoms they told us to expect, none of them were apparent with Deuce. He took things one day at a time, continuing to excel in school, playing basketball and enjoying life. He returned home feeling great and eager to get back to Memphis to conquer another round of treatment. Who knew in the weeks ahead, things would look very different?

The pain had begun to set in, and the once always positive diagnosis began to present new challenges to overcome. I found courage in family and friends, but I knew to depend on the power of God. I also had a warrior of a son who never complained, never got down on himself and always reminded us that he was good, that God had him. So, the question remained, what do you do when God tells you "no"? The more we prayed and asked God to heal him on this side, the more his sickness progressed. We prayed and fasted diligently expecting healing for Deuce. While discussing the process with Deuce, I spoke in basketball terms. I expressed we had shot all the shots we could shoot, but that was okay because we were now playing defense. We had our "Man in the paint" blocking every shot the adversary took. We deeply believed He would pull us through. I begged our God to leave my son with me.   We followed God's Holy Word and still God said "NO". I always uttered to Deuce the lyrics "I don't believe He brought me this far to leave me", that Deuce leaving was part of the plan.

I still wonder what I'm supposed to do when God tells you no. I may not ever know the correct answer, but I still pray with a "yes" expectancy. He knows my heart is broken and that I do not understand. However, I will serve and trust Him understanding He knows best. He has left me with the same task I stated in the beginning, to protect, provide and prepare not only my daughter but to do my part for all of God's children. I will continue to live by Deuce's words of expectancy and let each of them know that it's Okay, God's got us.

The Reluctant Father
Irvin A. Walker

When I was growing up, I wanted to pitch for the Chicago Cubs. As I got older, I wanted to coach basketball and teach History, Government/Economics, and Journalism. I never had a desire to be a Father. Life doesn't go as planned. God has other plans for your life. Some people call that Providence.

I never got an opportunity to teach the Motion Offense and help-side defense. Today, I am Television Producer/Director. I am, also, Father of four children. I have three daughters and a son, funny how things work out. George Washington was right; Providence can change history and it changed my life.

My wife and I have been together for almost 28 years. When our oldest daughter was born, I had absolutely no clue about how to change a diaper or be a father. 30 minutes after my daughter was born, I was taught how to put a diaper on her. I have been learning ever since. It was quite an experience being a dad for the first time. I never thought it would affect me, but it did. During those early days of parenthood, I found myself in challenging and frustrating situations. My wife would tell me what I needed to do and I felt it was easy when she was home. When she went back to work and then it was just me and daughter #1, Bianca that is when it became difficult. This is when you must step up, as a father, and do your job. Bianca and I got to know each other during those times. Soon, I was comfortable changing diapers, making formulas, dressing her, preparing diaper bags and going out in stroller to the store or church. I also took her to school, just like my dad did with me.

My younger brother and I grew up with both of our parents. They were both school teachers. They both stressed education, going to church, and staying out of trouble. As time went on, I went to Indiana State and got a degree in Radio-TV/Film. Then I moved to Columbia and went to work at Public Television. I met my wife and we got married. Pretty simple, then Bianca was born and we/I adjusted to having a new person in our lives. Being a father is an adjustment that you are going to make whether you want to or not. I found this time to be the most challenging period of my life.

Fast forward to 1998, my wife asked me what I thought about having another child. She said think about it. I said, "OK, I think that's a good idea!" I told her the reason for my quick response, "In my opinion, everything went well with Bianca, let's have another!" Erin was born later in 1999. The new challenge was to get to know Erin, like I did with Bianca. As time went on, I became more relaxed with the job of being a parent. I found myself relating more with Bianca because every day I took her to school. We would listen to the radio in the car, watch Rugrats, read, and I would help chaperone her field trips. Erin was still a baby. My wife was with her a lot. As time went on, Erin gravitated to her mother. I loved Erin. Erin presented a challenge that Bianca was not. At a young age, Erin was defiant. She wanted to do what she wanted to do. Erin taught me something that I was lacking in my own life. Patience. I learned patience with Erin. Erin wanted to do things her way and I wanted to do things my way. So, I learned how to compromise with her. I was still the dad, but I learned that I needed to be patient with BOTH of girls. I needed to understand that this wasn't about me; it was about your children. It was about, me, showing my girls the right way to do things and being patient enough to let them learn and grow on their own. That was a hard thing for me to do. It is still hard today.

Jumping forward to 2002, daughter #3 entered my life. Now, the man who wanted to be the next Spike Lee had become the man with 3 daughters. After Gabrielle was born, the first thought was how did we get here. My wife and I were thrilled on becoming parents for a third time. Several nights I would fall asleep thinking, "how am I going to put three girls through college, pay for three weddings, and how am I going to get through this?" Now there were four females in the Walker house. I felt like I was a living and breathing Walter Mosley book "Always Outnumbered".

Providence once again, touched me in way I never imagined. I always said, "Thank God I never had a son!" I could never imagine having a son. I figured since I have three girls, I doubt I would ever have a son. I was fine with that. I was very content on Vonda and me raising three girls and getting on with our lives. I was very happy with the family I had. I was still working in Television Production. I enjoyed what I was doing. My family I had was healthy. All was good, I thought, until my faith was tested. Twice.

In 2004, my son was born. He was born premature. He was in the hospital for several weeks. During the same time, my wife was became ill and, she too, was in the hospital. It was a very, very difficult time for me, personally. Professionally, I was working on a project that was very big in scope. I was the one of the Associate Producers and I was the main video editor of the project. It was an enormous task. At the same time, my wife and my new born son were in the hospital. Those days were, very difficult because I would have them on my mind, have my work responsibilities on my mind AND I had to care for Bianca, Erin, and Gabrielle. Things worked out fine; everyone recovered and is doing well. My faith wavered during that time in my life, but through it all, it became much stronger. My son and I have a nice relationship. We talk. We talk about things that happen in school, world news, and what he wants to do when he graduates high school. I like his aspirations.

We also communicate. He tells me when I "get on his nerves". I tell him "that's my job!" I listen to him and back off when it is needed and in that regard we have a nice father and son relationship. I always thought I would be Sgt. Hartman from "Full Metal Jacket", a drill sergeant. I guess I am not.

Most of my children are out of the house. They have gone on with their lives. A couple are still at home and getting ready for the next part of the journey in their lives. Vonda and I look forward to the next chapter in our lives. That chapter is having grown children. I never ever thought I would have four children. I never ever thought I would be a good dad due to my lack of patience. I had a good role model. I had a good teacher. I had a good dad. I hope I am as good a dad, to my children, as mine was to me and my brother. I think that was my fear, I did not know how to be a good parent. There is no book to give step by step instructions. I felt I could not be a good father because I did not know what to do. I guess I did know what to do, because I watched my dad for 25 years. He must have done something right.

In my opinion, to be a good dad, you have to be there from the time they are born until the day you die. You will change diapers, help with homework, show them how tie a tie, google where oil changing stores are located, and drive (2 ½ hours roundtrip) to your daughter's college to bring her winter clothes. It was all worth it in the long run, even if I never coached a game of basketball or made a feature film.

I named this essay, "The Reluctant Father". I felt I was reluctant because I had no clue about Fatherhood. I had a dad. True. I never asked about Fatherhood, I really did not know if I could be a good dad. People say you learn about fatherhood by watching your own father. I always though I didn't pay attention to my dad. In hindsight, I did, I just did not know it.

Letter To My Son
Rev. Torrey Woods

Son: Dad, Who am I?

Dad: You are a child of God and you are designed to be great.

Son: If that expectation is the case, then what does it take to be great?

Dad: Exodus 20:12 tells us that we must respect those who govern over us. Son, being well-disciplined and honorable will allow you to receive the wisdom and knowledge from those who have walked before you.

Son: What would my walk look like in the future?

Dad: There will be days where your walk will be easy and things will go your way. On the other hand, there will be days where trials and tribulations will come your way. However, in all things, whether good or bad, acknowledge God in all of you're doing and HE will direct your path.

Son: I think I understand what you are saying.

Dad: I am proud of you and I know that when you trust and believe in God, you will be GREAT. So go out there and tackle your dreams and goals and remember that I am rooting for you to succeed. Always stay prepared, because when you are prepared, you do not have to get prepared.

Son: Okay, Dad!

Dad: I Love You Son……

Never Knew My Father
John Sells

As a child growing up, all I knew was having a mom, four brothers and one sister at home. I am next to the last in this sibling order. My childhood was good growing up. Living with an older sister and brother, I never questioned where my dad was. From what I gathered, we were a functional working family. As I got older, I did question where was dad. The response was simply, "He left us". I did not feel any pain or guilt of not knowing him. I just assumed he left and started another life and I continued on with mine. My mom was more like a dad and mom combined. She had the most influence in my life to become the father and man I am today. She was strict, passionate, spiritual, loving and kind. She is where I got my attributes of being a good husband and father to my wife and kids.

When I left home single and joined the military, I eventually met my wife. When we planned to have kids, I felt prepared and ready to nourish my babies to adulthood. I credit my mom for how prepared I felt to become a father.

Being a father of four girls and one boy who had different attitudes and perspectives, I know my hands were going to be full. Being a father, I tried to raise my kids to respect themselves and others. I always taught them that manners will take them where money cannot.

But the most important thing that I instilled in them was to know God. That's a lesson which is worth a million dollars. Unfortunately, I wasn't taught that lesson during my childhood. In addition to teaching my kids about God, I tried to teach them other values. I want them to know how important it is to work for the things they want. I was a stickler for them to get an education. I encouraged them to not up give when facing disappointments.

In conclusion, I always want my kids to see me as a positive and communicative father. I'm proud that I was always present to love and take care of them. My goal was to raise them so they can go forward as lights to the world. I'm glad that I didn't let the fact that I never knew my father keep me from being a good father to them.

A Portrait of Fatherhood: Commitment, Engaged, and Loving
Dr. Nikolai Vitti

Of all of my responsibilities as a human being, leader, and citizen I have the greatest sense of pride, purpose, and duty in raising my four children with my best friend, and wife, Rachel.

Although I have some strong and lasting memories that have positively shaped my understanding of fatherhood through my own father's interaction with me, I also live daily with wounds of abandonment and longing after my parents separated and his decision to leave the area when I was young.

As I raise our children and problem solve through their natural challenges in life, observe their successes, failures and their development as people and future leaders, I question why he was not there? So many conversations did not take place; his love, acceptance, voice, touch, guidance, and strength was missing...lost...not there. I have come to understand that ambition, fear, conflict with my mother, and immigrant status all influenced the separation but none of that justifies my pain, what I needed as a young man.

Despite that pain, I have used it to fuel my own commitment to my own children and the 50,000 I have the privilege of serving as superintendent. In the end, when my life is considered, analyzed, and is retold by others, I live daily to never allow my own children, my family, and the greater community not to say that I was an engaged, present, demanding but loving father.

Portrait of Fatherhood
Essay Contributors

Levonia Butch Belt

Rev. Belt is involved in ministry in Anthem, Arizona.

For relaxation, he enjoys watching and playing basketball.

His reason for participating this project is to share a different point of view not often discussed.

The goal of his essay is to convey the point that no matter what your beginning, you will become what you want to be, not what your beginnings are.

Essay Title: Stability

Richard T. Benson

Dr. Benson is currently an Associate Professor of Clinical Neurology at Georgetown University Medical Center.

His hobbies include: reading, writing, movies, music, jogging, hiking, singing and volunteering. He resides in Washington, D.C.

Richard has always been inspired by the power of words. He believes that the ability to move people with words is an innate talent that can be developed only with years of training and life experiences.

The goal of his essay was to convey a unique view of the wide range of fathers and fatherhood, through the eyes of someone who struggled with ideas of societal and cultural norms, sexual identity and middle-class economics.

Essay Title: A Lesson In Life

Reverend Dr. Timothy "Tee" Boddie

Rev. Boddie is a Clergy and a Denominational Executive General Secretary of the Progressive National Baptist Convention

A self-professed trivia buff, Dr. Boddie also likes reading, writing, traveling, and cooking.

A Fisk University classmate of his wife introduced this book project to Rev. Boddie. As a Morehouse man and father, he felt he has a unique responsibility to define manhood for his own son and daughter, as well as for the next generations.

"Tee" feels strongly that it is an honor to share in the ongoing conversation about what it means to be a man in a world that falsely connects masculinity primarily with physical strength.

Essay Title: Man Up!

Marty B. Bulger

Mr. Bulger lives in Detroit, Michigan and works as an educator. During his career, he has been recognized as the Michigan Alternative Education Organization Administrator of the Year in 2014, and the Southfield Public Schools Partnership Council Administrator of the Year in 2014. When he is not working, he enjoys writing, music and weightlifting. Concerning his essay, Marty would like for all the readers to know how rewarding and priceless the simple things of fatherhood are and can be if only they would take the time to look. This is the pride of the price of the God-given opportunity to be impactful in the lives of our children.

Marty is the creative founder of this book project

Essay Title: Blessed To Be A Blessing

Terry E. Carter

Mr. Carter is a Non-Profit Manager and Communications Consultant who lives in Randolph, MA. He is also the author of three books of poetry, *Brown Skins and the Bread of Life* (2010), *Brown Skin and the Beautiful Faith* (2014) and *Brown Skin and the Brand New Day* (2016). (www.brownskinnedpoet.net)

For enjoyment, he loves writing poetry, painting, and collecting Black sports memorabilia. Terry agreed to join in this book project because he wanted to support a fellow Fisk University Alum who solicited his participation. Also, he agreed with the purpose of this project to bring the positive aspects of Black fatherhood to light, as he's tried to do in his own books of poetry.

Poem Title: Hero Mine

Billy D. Coker

Mr. Coker is a correctional officer who lives and works in Columbia, South Carolina. He is a member of the Trinity Baptist Church where he serves as Deacon and advisor to the Prison Ministry.

He enjoys basketball, smooth jazz, photography and just "hanging out" with family and friends.

Working in the prison system, Billy sees too often the plight of young men and boys not having a father figure in their lives. This is what inspired him to write the essay titled **Being There.**

He hopes that readers will understand the importance of just **Being There** that can make a difference in a child's life.

Essay Title: Being There

Dr. Omari Daniel

Omari Daniel is an English teacher who resides in Columbia, MD. In his spare time, he likes to fish, play chess, write poetry, and love his family.

After writing **We Fish the Journey to Fatherhood** with my father Jack Daniel, Omari realized it had been many years since he spoke on the subject. His sons Javon 17 and Deven 15 have grown up since then and the need to impart the wisdom he gained was a necessity, not an option. It was then he agreed to submit an essay to this book project.

Omari would like this essay to challenge each dad who reads it to become a little bit better by giving all of himself to his children. He hopes his writing will encourage them to find as many ways as they can to demonstrate that they are men worthy of being in the fraternity of fatherhood.

Poem Title: Real Fathers

Reggie Dokes

Reggie, a resident of Locust Grove, GA, is a World DJ/Music Producer of house, techno and hip-hop music. He runs his own house label, Psychostasia Recordings.

Mr. Dokes likes reading books dealing with history, finances and self-help in his spare time. He also enjoys gardening and collecting vinyl records.

Reggie agreed to submit an essay to this book project when he was invited to participate by his friend and brother, Marty Bulger. Marty is like a big brother to him who he loves and respects.

Mr. Dokes wants the readers of his essay to understand there are men who appreciate fatherhood. There are men who exist that believe fatherhood is a blessing and not a curse.

Poem Title: Blessed Fatherhood

Rev. James W. Gladden

Rev. Gladden is a United States Army Religious Affairs Specialist who resides in Platte City, Missouri. In his spare time, he likes to read, lift weight, watch football, and vacation with family.

He joined this book project because he felt it is very imperative to help men face the challenges of becoming a father that he have faced. WE cannot become stronger without assisting one another through the process.

Rev. Gladden wants the readers of his essay to understand that it is okay not to know what you are doing in the beginning. However, it is not okay to not give it your all to become a better father over time.

Essay Title: Developing the Father in You

Carlos A. Jones

Originally from Columbia, SC, Carlos currently resides in Charlotte, NC. He works as a Food Safety Manager for a well-recognized global snack brand.

Mr. Jones is a bourbon and cigar aficionado who also enjoys listening to and discussing music, reading, and listening to podcasts. He is active in Big Brother Big Sisters of Greater Charlotte and is very passionate about mentoring young African-American men.

Carlos joined this book project for several reasons. He is passionate about fatherhood and he enjoys writing. It it is important to him that others outside of our community understand that the myth of the invisible Black father is just that-a myth.

From his essay, Mr. Jones hopes the reader gets that being a present, engaged and loving father in a blended family situation is possible.

Essay Title: Two Homes, One Heart

Milton Jones, Jr.

Reggie, Milton is a teacher who resides in Farmington Hills, MI.
For enjoyment, he likes to bike riding, exercising and coaching football.
Mr. Jones believes that one the biggest accomplishments in his life is being a father. He had a great role model in his father to show him the way.
From his essay, he hopes his readers see how much he loves his father and how highly he values the role of being a father now.

Essay Title: Real Fathers

Robert A. Martin, PhD

A resident of Rochester Hills, MI, Dr. Martin is a retired public-school teacher and administrator. Currently, he is a Visiting Assistant Professor at Oakland University in Educational Leadership. His hobbies include music, traveling, reading, and trying new restaurants. After 28 years, he retired as the Artistic Director of Madrigal Chorale, a semi-professional chorus in the metropolitan Detroit area.

Fatherhood has been a double-edged sword throughout Robert's life. In childhood, fatherhood represented a hole in his heart. In young adulthood, fatherhood represented a mystery and then a quest. In his twilight years, fatherhood is one of his greatest sources of fulfillment, struggle, and joy. Primarily, Robert wants the readers of his essay to know that fathers are important and necessary! No matter the circumstance or age, our children need us. Moreover, we need them. Each fatherhood path is unique. Full of adventure, missteps and triumphs. Enjoy the journey.

Essay Title: Just As I Am

Gregory A. Montgomery II

Mr. Montgomery works in I.S. Team Computer Analysis. He resides in Detroit, Michigan.

For enjoyment, he likes British Cars, Japanese Motorcycles and 100-year-old Homes of Detroit's Historic Boston-Edison District.

Gregory joined this book project because he was asked to submit his thoughts by his fraternity brother of Phi Beta Sigma Fraternity, Inc.

He wants the reader to know that we are just links in a chain and that we must impart the legacy given to us to the future generations of Black men to follow so as to not repeat the same mistakes…

Essay Title: One Hundred Words on Fatherhood

Kenneth Maurice Moore

Kenneth is a lawyer and business owner who lives in Los Angeles, California. He enjoys writing, reading, and playing various sports.

Concerning the inspiration to write, Mr. Moore recalls a fall day as a *"pretentious third grader"* when his teacher gave him and the other students a challenging writing assignment. That was the day the seeds of his writing career were planted.

Kenneth attributes his current inspiration to his fiancé and soulmate Sheila Hudson and says with a smile that he hopes to one day be the best writer in his own home.

Essay Title: What's The Matter With White People: Finally, I Believe I See

Kevin Morgan

Kevin is an author of 9 books and an entrepreneur who resides in Columbia, SC. He is also the owner of a publishing company, Sowjourn Publishers.

He is an avid reader, preferably books by African-American authors. Also, he likes to listen to jazz music, cook, frame artwork, and perform community service.

As an author, Kevin welcomes the challenges of sharing information in an enjoyable and informative way for his readers. As a publisher, he likes helping other authors communicate their thoughts and opinions.

In his essay, Kevin wants the readers to empathize with fathers who struggle with the outcomes of the choices they've made concerning their children.

Kevin served as the editor and publisher of this book.
Essay Title: The Least

Jerome S. Nesbitt

Mr. Nesbitt is a Philanthropy Officer with The American Red Cross who resides in Columbia, SC.

In his spare time, he enjoys playing golf, coaching youth basketball, and listening to music.

Jerome considered it an honor to join this book project. It has given him a platform to share thoughts that have been bottled up inside him for a long time. Hopefully his inclusion in this process will encourage others to search for answers that have eluded them.

He hopes that after reading this book, readers will be reminded that it's okay to question God and ask for an expected outcome. They may never get a clear answer or understanding to all questions, but they will find comfort in knowing that God is sovereign, and His will is always done.

Essay Title: A Father's Test of Faith-What Do You Say When God Says No?

Dana Keone O'Banion

Mr. O'Banion is an attorney who lives and works in Chicago, IL. He also the author of *"Squirrelly the Squirrel"*, a children's book. An avid jogger, Dana also enjoys working with youths as a coach and mentor as well as reading.

He was first inspired to write when he and his young sons encountered a haggard looking squirrel in the park. From that encounter came his children's story. Writing this piece is inspired by the love he has for his sons and the potential he sees in all children.

Dana hopes readers of his essay understand that parenting can be very fun. It is a great responsibility and honor to raise children. Parents should be relentless and deliberate in "**RAISE**"ing children.

Essay Title: Fatherhood

Dathon O'Banion

A resident of Chicago, Il, Dathon is an Insurance and Financial Services professional who specializes in Retirement Planning.

Dathon likes road cycling and research of things that have impacted or will impact the world we live in. He also likes spending time trying to help his special needs APBT *"get right"*.

When Mr. O'Banion saw the first edition of this book project, he thought it par excellent. So, when he was asked to contribute an essay, he felt some of what he shared with his children might benefit others.

Through his essay, Dathon wants the reader to understand that sibling rivalries should not trump the ethos of sibling love and camaraderie.

Essay Title: A Statement on Friendship to Sons

John Sells

John Sells is a retired Master Sergeant from the Army who lives in Columbia, SC.

His hobbies include walking, fishing and watching sports.

Mr. Sells agreed to submit an essay to this book project because he wanted others to learn from his experiences of growing up without his father. He wanted to be an asset that others can draw from to guide them in their respective fatherhood journeys.

John hopes the readers of his essay will be able to accept they can adjust to and overcome anything that might hinder them from becoming a good father.

Essay Title: Never Knew My Father

Bruce W. Strouble, Sr.

Mr. Strouble is retired and lives in Columbia, SC.

His hobbies include writing, singing, fishing, and spending time with family.

Bruce believes his poem fits in exactly with the purpose of this book project. He originally wrote this piece to be presented at a Father's Day program in Pasadena, California several years ago. So, when this project and the purpose of it was mentioned to him, he felt that this poem spoke perfectly to the cause.

In its simplicity, this poem asks all fathers and those young men who will be fathers to give their best to their children, and particularly, to their sons.

Poem Title: A Better Portion

Michael R. Twyman, Ph.D.

Dr. Twyman is a Social Entrepreneur/Scholar who lives in Indianapolis, IN.

In his spare time, Michael enjoys running marathons, cycling, traveling abroad, and public speaking.

The reason he agreed to contribute an essay was because he wanted to add his voice to the stories of other men on the importance of fatherhood. He believes our collective experiences might provide inspiration and hope for our communities.

Dr. Twyman wants the readers of his essay to be encouraged and empowered by striving to live a life with purpose and self-discipline, both of which only come with practice, patience, and sacrifice.

Essay Title: Words of Wisdom

Dr. Nikolai Vitti

Dr. Nikolai Vitti is the Superintendent of Detroit Public Schools.

Essay Title: A Portrait of Fatherhood: Commitment, Engaged, and Loving

Irwin Walker

Irwin Walker is a Television Producer/Director/Writer in Columbia, SC

In his spare time, his hobbies include history, astronomy, smooth jazz, cooking and reading.

He was inspired to write this essay because he liked a challenge. Being a father was a challenge that he reluctantly accepted and he wanted to use this essay to tell why he was hesitant.

Mr. Walker hopes that the readers of his essay will understand that there is no wrong or right way to parent. He wants the reader to know that parenting never stops. The responsibility is enormous, but rewarding.

Essay Title: The Reluctant Father

Oscar J Walker, III

Oscar Walker is Retired from State Government / US Army Reserves. He is also a Consultant with Jermaine Enterprises. He resides in Columbia, SC.

His interests include anything that relates to family history and the welfare of Black youth.

Mr. Walker chose to participate in this book project because he wanted to express his strong interest in fatherhood. His focus is on raising a Black male youth. In his opinion, we only have one institution that has empirical data on our Black youth which is the Law Enforcement and Prison systems.

In his opinion, it's up to the Black family, church and community to correct the attitude of our Black youth in communities that have high dropout rates, shootings, negative attitudes and disrespect. In his essay, he hopes the reader get the point made in raising his son; it still "takes a village".

Essay Title: How Do I Portray Fatherhood?

Gary A. Williams

Mr. Williams, who resides in Detroit, MI, is a Sales Director at the Boy Scouts of America. He also is a semi-retired pastor.

In his spare time, Gary's hobbies include housing rehabilitation, reading, writing and public speaking.

As the father of three sons, and the sixth son of his parents, Mr. Williams believes this has given him some insight into being the father of sons. His life's work has been punctuated with being an advocate for youth, especially Black males. When he was asked to contribute an essay for this project, he jumped at the opportunity.

Gary hopes the reader will value at least three assertions that are presented in his essay.

1. What a father does is the best example a father can set.
2. Being present allows your values to be transferred both consciously and sub-consciously.
3. The lives of a father and his sons should be built upon a spiritual foundation

Essay Title: Fatherhood: A Sacred Responsibility

Kevin E. Wimberly

Mr. Wimberly is President/CEO of SC UpLift Community Outreach, a non-profit corporation.

In his spare time, Kevin enjoys spending time with family, watching sports and working-out.

He joined the book project because he saw it as an opportunity to pay homage to his grandfathers, but mostly his father.

Kevin would like the readers of his essay to understand that he doesn't take for granted the legacy of his grandfathers and father. Fatherhood is not easy but reflecting on the life they lived is inspirational to know that other men can be successful fathers.

Essay Title: A Father's Legacy

Rev. A. Torrey Woods

Rev. Woods is a Minister and Life Coach who resides in Chandler, Arizona. His hobbies include coaching, teaching and travelling.

His reason for agreeing to submit an essay to this book was to show a positive enlightenment to young Black youths.

From his essay, Rev. Woods hopes his readers see how a father takes the time to communicate with his son in the hope of giving him wisdom nuggets that will lead him to becoming successful.

Essay Title: Dear Son